The Happiness Workbook For Women

Practical Strategies to Get Unstuck, Stay Positive and Find Inner Peace - Includes 15 Challenges to Trigger Your Happiness Every Day

Victoria Tyler

Table of Contents

INTRODUCTION

As a woman, I was expected to study, get good grades, graduate, find a good-paying job, and get married and have a family. So that's what I did. I was the model daughter and student. I found a well-paying job after graduation and got married. But along the way, I realised that something wasn't right. I WASN'T HAPPY.

This got me thinking: what if following the set prerequisites but finding the man of your life, getting married, and having kids does not mean happiness for not just me but all the women out there? What if working a nine-to-five job does not give you the satisfaction you are looking for? What if as a woman, you feel restricted and the gender differences in society are stifling your happiness?

And if these things are all you could or would want to do, how can you do them and be happy? If this is everything you are feeling right now, you are not alone! I have been through all these struggles myself, and I personally know of more women like you and me. Between trying to find love, being successful at work or school, and fitting into a society that will not accept you unless you conform to its rules, I felt frustrated and far from happy.

I set out to discover happiness and discovered the lessons I am about to describe here. I will help you find purpose in all these things to make the right changes to help you find happiness. This workbook will serve as a support for your mental wellbeing and help you rekindle the happiness in everything you do in life. From meditation to daily schedules, this workbook will teach you to rewire your brain, surround yourself with positive people, and choose the positive over negative.

If you think that being happy is something you are born with, this workbook is here to change that opinion. Happiness is a state of mind. I will help channel your inner child, and just like children, we will rediscover joy in its raw form. If, like me, you have always wished for a happier life and struggled with this mindset, this workbook will explain happiness, look into it in different life situations, and teach you how to choose it in ten simple steps.

Women chase after materialistic things with the aim of being happy when those things are in hand, but it is fleeting happiness. This workbook is intended to teach you how to be happy with or without these things. Everyone thinks about happiness and wants it for themselves and their loved ones. Everyone is surrounded by social media and bombarded with expectations of happiness, but what few of us realize is that it can be defined in different ways; it varies based on one's perspective. A lot of people, me included, aspire to be happy and have their own idea of how this may be achieved.

One of the most basic requirements of a living being is to be happy. Mankind has been attempting to invent new technologies and create new tools to better one's lifestyle with the sole aim of achieving happiness since the start of civilization. On the other hand, people are hardly conscious of what truly defines happiness in the race to attain new scientific endeavors while chasing money and self-indulgence.

It's when negative stress levels are at their lowest, if not absent, that positivity improves a person's emotions. The objective of nations and societies is to make people happy. Happy people have been found to be more successful at work and to spread positive energy to others. Happiness is an intangible that cannot be achieved through material possessions. Although worldly objects may temporarily increase happiness, they only do so for a limited time. Our idea of happiness is shaped by our state of mind and senses.

Before you start working through this workbook, be aware that there will be suggestions and challenges that may seem ludicrous or contradictory to your objectives. However, the activities will help you on your journey to discovering happiness. You're required to figure out what you want out of life.

This workbook does not encourage you to give up or stop working. but rather it sets forth a strategy to focus on more important things and train your mind to do so. It is about breaking the bad habits that have evolved in one's life. Together, we will investigate everything that constitutes true happiness. The chapters will examine the blunders people make in their pursuit of happiness, as well as the misconceptions that surround the concept. I will go through how to be happier in life as well as several ways to track your progress.

I encourage you to accept the challenges listed in this book and the tips suggested throughout. They may seem like baby steps, but they will help you reflect and positively affect your level of happiness. The scope of the workbook is to gain control over your life, find the "happy" in everything, and always choose happiness.

This is not an easy mission, especially if you have been taught to contain your excitement from a young age, always being told what to do to be happy on everyone else's terms.

If you often experience anxiety, depression, sadness, low self-esteem and self-worth, this guide will help you deal with these emotions instead of avoiding them. Instead of brushing these emotions off, you will learn to deal with them because, they are almost inevitable. By the end of this workbook, you will have better control over your moods. You will wake up in a more exciting state of mind daily with less stress and anxiety.

Overall, the process will increase your level of life satisfaction. If you feel you are not able to achieve this right now, do not worry I will work with you. If you feel after the loss of someone you loved that you will never experience happiness again, do not feel discouraged. If you feel you do not belong at the job you currently have and you will never fit in anywhere, be hopeful. I will outline numerous ways to find happiness again, and everything else will follow. Be sure to keep your targets in mind, and you will most definitely tick them off by the end of the workbook.

I am very looking forward to sharing this journey with you to help you find happiness and leverage the joyous moments in your life as a woman!

CHAPTER 1: WHAT DEFINES HAPPINESS?

Happiness is characterized by a feeling of pleasure, but this can be hard to define. What defines "happiness" for you? What, in your opinion, makes people happy? Do you believe happiness can be quantified or do you believe it is subjective, as some argue? Because happiness, to me, is a subjective notion, its definition varies from person to person.

Money is all that matters to certain people when it comes to happiness. For some, simply listening to their favorite song may suffice. It could be reading a book for you. As a result, everyone's notion of happiness is unique. The state of the feeling of happiness, on the other hand, is the same. As a result, the methods for accomplishing it are more or less typical.

The Happy Hormones

Before we dive into the exercises and start the journey to happiness, there is some crucial information you need to know about happiness. Happy chemicals including serotonin, dopamine, oxytocin, and endorphins are well-known to promote pleasant emotions like pleasure, happiness, and even love. Hormones and neurotransmitters have a key role in a variety of vital functions, including heart rate, digestion, mood, and feeling regulation.

They are the chemical messengers of the body, and some are recognized for assisting people in bonding, feeling joy, and experiencing pleasure. Understanding the significance of these happy chemicals in the brain and body, as well as their impact on mental health, allows you to take proactive measures to naturally elevate their levels.

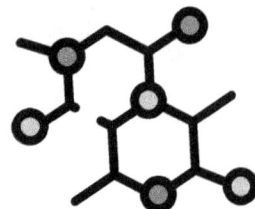

To put it another way, happy hormones equal a happier version of yourself. I will not tire you with the science stuff; however, I feel that identifying the hormones important for happiness and their roles is crucial to understand happiness and how to enhance it.

Hormones are substances produced by various glands throughout the human body, and their primary role is to communicate between two glands or a gland and an organ. Throughout the day, your body's hormones rise and fall. Cortisol, for example, wakes you up in the morning, while melatonin, another hormone, helps you get ready for bed in the evening. The hormones that inform you when you're hungry, full, happy, or unhappy are also important.

The endocrine system regulates the production and release of hormones into the bloodstream. It's a system of glands that runs all across the body. Hormones play a role in mood control, pleasure, bonding, and even pain alleviation. That isn't all, though. These molecules are important for growth and development, metabolism, and reproduction, among other things.

These hormones are also known as neurotransmitters. Except for where they act, there isn't much of a distinction between hormones and neurotransmitters. Happy hormones circulate in the bloodstream to many organs and tissues, but happy neurotransmitters are found only in the brain and central nervous system, where they communicate directly with neurons.

Many feel-good hormones exist in the body to increase mood and promotes overall wellbeing in a variety of ways. Some help with worry and depression, while others help with pleasure, joy, connecting, and trust. Serotonin is a mood stabilizer and is involved with wellbeing and happiness. Dopamine is a chemical involved with pleasure and plays an important part in the reward system of the brain, together with motivation. Oxytocin affects bonding, love, and trust.

Endorphins

Endorphins are chemicals that affect pain relief and relaxation. Happiness hormones reflect your surroundings, relationships, nutrition, exercise routine and, in certain situations, even your gut microorganisms, which is less well recognized. It's true: the decisions you make every day have the capacity to alter your mood. In this book, we will look at how to do that.

Endorphins make you feel good, but not in the way you think. Endorphins are hormones and neuro-signaling molecules that function like painkillers. They bind to opioid receptors, which are the body's natural morphine and block the transmission of pain signals in the central nervous system.

These hormones, known as neurotransmitters, participate in producing a cheerful mood and positive feelings. Serotonin, for example, is also known as the happiness hormone, while dopamine is known as the feel-good hormone, and oxytocin is known as the cuddle hormone. The gut microbiome contributes to the generation of neurotransmitters such as dopamine and serotonin.

These not only allow neurons to interact with one another but also link the neurological and digestive systems. To put it another way, a happy gut equals a happy mind! There are several natural ways to raise your mood, emotions, and even cognitive function by increasing your levels of dopamine, serotonin, and oxytocin. Exercising, sharing a meal with loved ones, and boosting your prebiotic and probiotic consumption are all excellent ways to do so.

Serotonin

Serotonin is required for mood, digestion, sleep, brain function, and circadian rhythm to function properly. Besides a healthy balanced diet, exercise has also been demonstrated to increase tryptophan and serotonin levels, which should come as no surprise.

It also helps to increase the diversity of the gut microbiome, which is good for your overall health.

Although you can't consume serotonin, there are two ways to increase serotonin through diet. To begin, include more prebiotic foods in your diet to help your beneficial bacteria thrive. Foods that feed your gut bacteria are apples, barley, root vegetables like beetroots, potatoes, and onions, berries, citrus fruits, mushrooms, garlic and wholewheat grains.

You can boost the amount of foods that naturally contain tryptophan, an essential amino acid the body requires to make serotonin. Just keep in mind that your body requires roughly 30 grams of fiber per day from meals, and that meat and fats should be consumed in moderation. This will aid in the equilibrium of your body and intestinal microorganisms. Food rich in tryptophan are sunflower seeds, grains like oats and what, spirulina, dairy products like milk and cheese, salmon, chicken, beef, and turkey.

Oxytocin

Oxytocin is the hormone in charge of promoting trust and bonding; it is especially active during delivery because it causes contractions. Its function as a neurotransmitter that helps control stress reactions and soothe the nervous system is one of its lesser-known but equally significant functions. Higher amounts of oxytocin in the blood have been related to increased feelings of love, attentiveness, and gratitude in couples.

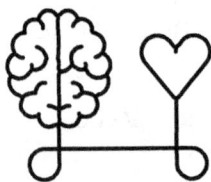

Oxytocin is secreted in reaction to cues detected by the brain and your senses to carefully monitor your environment for threats and indicators of safety. It is also produced during stressful moments to counteract cortisol's effects.

Oxytocin is released when you experience a caring relationship and surround yourself with a loving community, whether it's a pet, a romantic relationship, or friends.

Dopamine

Dopamine is another hormone that keeps you alive and alert, while also making you feel pleased. It's involved in a wide range of functions, and dopamine deficiency has been linked to a number of serious illnesses. Dopamine is responsible for motor controls, the brain's motivation system, and the reward system. Dopamine is involved in the decision-making process and impulse control. Dopamine also helps with memory and attention. Finally, this is also involved in maternal and reproductive behaviors. This is normally released when you either think of food or eat your favorite meal.

Measuring Happiness

Some say that happiness should not be the topic of scientific investigation since it is hard to evaluate it objectively. People are happy if they believe they are, and everyone is the best judge of whether they are truly happy. Happiness is a construct that may be scientifically examined through qualitative and quantitative assessment, even though it is difficult to define.

Happiness is studied in many ways by psychologists. Need and Goal Satisfaction Theories are among the results. According to these ideas, pleasure is the outcome of pursuing appropriate goals and achieving one's basic human needs. These state that happiness is attained when autonomy, competence, and belonging, are met.

What do you consider important needs that must be met in order for you to achieve happiness? List them below.

_____

_____

_____

_____

List three of your strengths that you feel contributes to your overall happiness in life.

List three of your flaws that you feel hinders your happiness overall.

While everyone defines happiness differently, there are major indicators that psychologists look for when evaluating and analyzing happiness. Some of these indicators include feeling like you're living the life you've always wanted, having the notion that your life is going well, and feeding the belief that you have or will achieve your goals in life.

If you're happy with your life, you are more optimistic than pessimistic. This is about perspective and if right now you are talking to yourself thinking how pessimistic you are most of the time, do not worry, I am here to change that. It's crucial to remember that happiness isn't a continual state of pleasure. Happiness, on the contrary, is a feeling of having more pleasant emotions than negative ones.

From time to time, happy people experience the full spectrum of human emotions, including anger, frustration, boredom, loneliness, and even grief. These people have an underlying sense of optimism that things will get better, they will be able to deal with what is occurring, and they will be able to be happy again, even while they are in discomfort. So, if when choosing this workbook, you thought that once finished you will be able to achieve happiness as a constant state, you were wrong.

If this was your target since forever, that is probably why you have struggled with happiness. I cannot promise you will never experience negative emotions in your life, but I can promise you that you can learn to deal with these in the best possible ways, without jeopardizing your state of happiness.

Different Types of Happiness

Happiness can be interpreted in a variety of ways. Aristotle, the ancient Greek philosopher, defined happiness in two ways. Pleasure is the source of hedonic bliss. It is most commonly connected with doing what makes you happy, self-care, fulfilling wants, having fun, and feeling satisfied. The pursuit of virtue and meaning gives rise to eudaimonia. Well-being is an important component of this, as is the sensation that your life has meaning, worth, and purpose.

It is closely related to carrying out responsibilities, investing in long-term goals, caring for the wellbeing of others, and living up to your own standards. Hedonia and eudemonia are now more often referred to as pleasure and meaning, respectively, in psychology. More recently, psychologists have proposed adding a third component relating to engagement. These are feelings of dedication and participation in several aspects of life.

According to research, joyful people have higher eudemonic life satisfaction and higher hedonic life satisfaction than ordinary people. Although the relative importance of each can be extremely subjective, they can all play an important influence on the overall feeling of happiness. Some hobbies are both joyful and significant, while others lean more toward one or the other.

As a personal example, when I volunteered for two weeks in Southeast Asia, my experience was more meaningful than pleasurable. The reason for this is because the experience itself was in line with my values. Watching my favorite TV show will have less meaning and more pleasure for me, and probably for you too. You may express happiness in the form of joy which would be a brief feeling that is felt in real-time.

Excitement is another way of expressing happiness, and it involves looking forward to something and anticipating positively. Gratitude is a positive feeling that involves feeling appreciative of what you have or being grateful for the present situation. Pride is also a feeling of happiness and satisfaction for things you have accomplished. Optimism is a positive way of looking at anything, including life in general. Contentment is a sense of satisfaction and is also classified as happiness.

Why do you need to choose happiness? If you are still trying to figure out WHY happiness deserves your time, attention, and energy, here is why:

- ☑ In many different areas of life, happiness has been found to predict favorable outcomes.

- ☑ Positive emotions improve life satisfaction.

- ☑ People with more happiness have better-coping skills and emotional resources.

- ☑ Positive emotions have been related to increased longevity and better health.

- ☑ Positive emotions make you more resilient. When people are resilient, they can better manage stress and bounce back from setbacks.

- ☑ People who report feeling confident in themselves are more likely to engage in healthy habits like eating healthy and exercising regularly.

- ☑ Being cheerful may assist you in becoming sick less frequently. Increased immunity is connected to happier mental states.

- ☑ The need for self-actualization, or realizing one's full potential, is at the top of Maslow's hierarchy of needs. Peak experiences of transcendent moments, in which a person feels deep insight, satisfaction, and joy, are also important, according to this theory. People are motivated to pursue increasingly complicated demands according to the hierarchy of needs. People are then motivated by greater psychological and emotional demands once their basic requirements have been met.

Some people can strike you as born happy. While you may not be able to alter the "general level" of happiness you were born with or taught, there are things you can do to make your life more enjoyable and satisfying. Even the happiest people might feel down from time to time, and happiness is something that everyone should strive for.

Write down three things you want to achieve after finishing this workbook.

WHY do you want to be happy?

_____

_____

_____

_____

List four things that make you happy. This could be anything from a weekend break to simply listening to your favorite song:

_____

_____

_____

_____

The following exercises will help you identify what is interfering with your happiness at any given time during the day, whether it is before going out to meet friends, or prior to going to bed.

Write down the first thing you think of, as soon as you wake up in the morning:

_____

_____

_____

_____

What is that one thing that is hindering your good night sleep or that is keeping you from sleeping at a decent time:

_____

_____

_____

_____

Have you tried meditating before but struggle because of the flow of thoughts that get to your head? Jot down a few of these thoughts below:

_____

_____

_____

_____

Does anxiety take over when you make plans to meet someone or get together with friends? How do you feel after committing to seeing someone ?

_____

_____

_____

_____

_____

_____

What worries you the most is deciding what to wear if someone you know will be there, and whether you will need a drink or two to loosen up. Will you be bored and have to make up excuses to leave early? Do you contemplate on canceling at the last minute to get out of it?

_____

_____

_____

_____

_____

_____

_____

◎ CHALLENGE 1

Contemplate on how you spend your week. List down the activities you do on any given day.

Sunday	Monday	Tuesday	Wednesday	Thursday	Friday	Saturday

After listing these activities, and they can be anything, including showering, sleeping, reading, or having lunch with your friends, take time to rate these activities. Use a gauge from one to five, with 1 being the least pleasurable activity.

By the end of this challenge, you should have reflected on your days and how you spend your time. The challenge for this activity is to focus on increasing the things you scored 5 on because these are the ones that give you the most joy and pleasure.

While some things may be a requirement, keep these in mind because I will be making such activities more pleasurable or acceptable.

For example, if now you are absolutely dreading work, it may still be a necessity because you may not be in a stable financial position to resign now and take a break from work, but there are ways to enjoy your work a bit more if leaving your current employment is not an option.

Joy, pleasure, contentment, and fulfillment characterize happiness as an emotional state. Simply put, the study of happiness investigates what makes individuals happy. When you think about it, the subjective nature of happiness makes it extremely difficult to define and quantify.

Since ancient Greece, happiness has been a source of debate and discussion. Happiness has been defined by science as the result of prioritizing pleasure over pain. When most people talk about happiness, they may be referring to how they feel right now, or they may be referring to a broader sense of how they feel about life in general.

Because happiness is such a broad concept, psychologists and other social scientists often refer to it as "relative wellbeing" when studying this emotional state. Relative wellbeing, as the name implies, is concerned with an individual's overall personal feelings about their current situation. All pleasures appear to involve the same brain circuits, from the most basic like eating and sexual pleasure to monetary, medical, and humanitarian rewards.

On my journey to happiness, the first was to define what happiness meant to me and that is exactly what the first task will be: "What does happiness mean to you?" And please note that here is a safe place. It doesn't matter what you write, no one will pass judgement. Therefore, be as honest with yourself as possible because honesty is another step in the journey.

Write down what is the meaning of happiness to you. Try to define it in a way as if you are explaining the meaning of it to someone that has never experienced it or has never known what it is:

_____

_____

_____

_____

_____

There are a lot of happiness myths like beautiful people are happier, rich people are happier, happiness is not a skill, and success can make you happy. You have purchased this book because despite striving to achieve the above-mentioned myths, you still struggle to feel happy or make happy a way of life.

There is probably a script surrounding your idea of happiness. For example, where I come from, the idea of happiness is studying, graduating, finding someone you shall love for the rest of your life, getting married and building a family with them, raise obedient kids in a loving home you have worked for all your life, and the life cycle repeats itself.

You may want to buy your ideal home is a great leap of success in your life, but you also need to get that new car model to feel fully happy. Once you acquire the car of your dreams, you may still miss one more thing to feel happy - a better paying job perhaps. I will work with you throughout this guide to help you overcome the mindset that happiness can only be achieved when you fulfill all your materialistic needs or goals.

Write down what would be the ideal formula for your happiness:

_____

_____

_____

_____

_____

_____

_____

_____

CHAPTER 2:
HAPPINESS IN DIFFERENT SPHERES OF LIFE

A lot of people make the mistake of developing one area of their life and forgetting about the rest. In this day and age, people are forced to focus on their finances and have a successful career. This may put the rest of the areas of their life at stake. Focusing just on careers and finances may mean that family, relationships, and health are ignored. This means that their family and romantic relation suffer, as well as their health.

Remember that if you want to be happy, you must grow in all areas. You may be more active in some areas and more passive in others, but you should set aside time for everything else for your own sake. I was always instructed to be successful at life I must have a successful career and must work hard for it.

The values I was taught in the process are the fundamentals by which I live today; however, because I was focused on one thing and ignored the rest, a lot of happiness in many aspects of my life was sacrificed. Perfecting my career meant I left no time for leisure, fun, or friends.

Everything we have is based on our physical and psychological well-being. You may not be able to accomplish anything in this life if you lack energy. Nature has given us the ability to move, do something, eat, and drink, but we must use it appropriately.

Regular exercise and proper nutrition are never-ending sources of health. This is why I make it a priority today, to leave time for myself, time to perform physical activity, whether it is a game of squash with a friend or a circuit training class.

Many successful people who may have become leaders and achieved success and fortune have been wrecked by alcohol and smoking. The house and its ambiance have a significant impact on a person's inner state, inspiring and relaxing them at the same time. Proper home space management can free up a lot of time for other things, especially for stay-home women who spend the most time in this area.

This came in particularly handy when I started working from home. Clearing out my space became a priority. Self-development is frequently overlooked and underutilized. Reading books, studying, attending special training events, master classes, acquiring skills, changing oneself, and giving up undesirable habits are all examples of this. One of my favourite is looking up books I would like to read and add them to my yearly book-reading challenge. I have never found so much pleasure in hovering through books at book fairs and finding what I want.

All of this is geared toward bettering yourself and reaching your objectives, as well as the desire to approach an ideal life. Communication skills, the ability to develop positive relationships with family and friends and the ability to interact with colleagues and friends are all aspects of human relations.

Everyone has their own assumption about what constitutes recreation and enjoyment. Rest means different things to different people. For some, it means spending time doing their favorite activity; for others, it means relaxing in a bath with essential oils; and for others, it means traveling to exotic places. Choose a profession that will provide you pleasure.

Our inner world has a big influence on how we set our goals and objectives. Emotions, stress resistance, motivation, and spiritual life are all part of it. It is vital to create a circle of life balance to analyze our lives in all its realms, appropriately define goals and objectives, correct mistakes, and attain harmony.

Happiness at Work

How often do you contemplate leaving your job because you believe you are underpaid for the devotion and service you provide to your company? Happiness and contentment are subjective ideas; while monetary rewards may be linked with job satisfaction for some, others may desire recognition of their efforts and lose motivation if they do not receive it.

For some people, having a pleasant work atmosphere is a must to enjoy themselves.

Whatever the standards, being satisfied with our jobs is essential for maintaining a healthy work-life balance. In its most basic form, workplace pleasure occurs when you love executing the tasks allocated to you and feel good about the people with whom you work. You are satisfied with the financial benefits you receive from your employment and could improve your current abilities.

Happiness arises when you are recognized and acknowledged. Workplace happiness is more than just a combination of smart investments and good returns. Personality qualities, the level of perception, underlying psychological pressures, and emotional intelligence all have an impact on how comfortable we feel in a professional setting.

There is a reason the concept of workplace happiness did not exist until a few decades ago. The industrial sector has changed dramatically in recent years, and we now work in roles that did not exist twenty years ago. In the 1940s, who would have imagined job titles like Social Media Manager, SEO Expert, Chief Happiness Officer, Motivational Coach, and Speaker, Career Counsellor, or Project Coordinator?

These posts are created because everyone recognizes the need for happiness and job commitment at work. With such a diverse choice of complex duties to choose from nowadays, it is critical that we can derive actual joy from the work we do. For a growing company, happy employees are a must. A cheerful employee will arrive at work on time because she values punctuality and will complete all the daily responsibilities because she enjoys them. She will work because she loves it, not because she must.

Workplace joy may spread like wildfire. Employees who enjoy what they do set a terrific example for others who are less motivated. When a team leader is satisfied with his job and work, for example, he can have a greater positive influence on his team and ensure that the group functions well. A professional with strong positive thoughts about his work will surely be more eager and focused on his own development.

Rather than focusing on issues, he would concentrate on how to solve them. We will never be able to get rid of work stress and disappointments if we allow them to enter our personal space. . Hypertension, cardiac arrests, substance misuse, and other stress-related diseases are less prevalent among successful professionals who maximize their work.

This should come as no surprise when working over eight hours a day makes up most of your day. You spend less time at home with family and friends than you do at work. When we are content on the inside, we have the strength to combat disease and the determination to recover and get back on track. Staying unwell, whether physically or emotionally, might put you at a disadvantage at work.

We lose the motivation to give it our all, become less focused on work and more focused on our problems; and as a result, our productive soul dies. Not only that, but enjoyment at work reduces our susceptibility to work-related stress and responsibilities.

Are you happy at work? How do you feel in the morning knowing you have a work-day ahead?

_____

_____

_____

_____

_____

Work was a chore where I grew up. My parents were often exhausted and irritated; they never felt financially comfortable enough to unwind. They felt defeated by work, overburdened by unrealistic demands, and hardened by a sense that no one else was pulling their weight. To top it off, no one appeared to notice or appreciate the enormous lengths to which people would go to get things just right.

I'm sure they aren't alone. It's common for 55 to 80 percent of us to view work as something to be endured rather than enjoyed. We work all day and then try to strike the perfect work-life balance at home, assuming that work is about stress and the rest of our lives are about actual happiness. That viewpoint, however, does not hold up under scientific investigation. In fact, data from psychology, leadership, and management studies, and even neuroscience supports a contrary viewpoint: that finding happiness at work is not only attainable but also beneficial.

Employees who are happier perform better on all fronts, from daily health to productivity to career progression, and this improves the bottom line for the company. So, how do we change our minds regarding work happiness? And how can you make your work lives feel more fulfilling, as though they are contributing meaningfully to our overall happiness?

I don't believe happiness is a fleeting emotional state like amusement, pleasure, or heartfelt pride is. Some do not believe happiness can be achieved by accumulating a series of positive events. Rather, they consider happiness to be an encompassing quality of life that is constituted of different emotions, including anger, sadness, and stress. While it's not ideal for these more difficult feelings to persist too long or have too much of an effect on how we think, the situations in which they occur are often what drive our deeper sense of purpose and bring us into meaningful touch with others.

I shall use comparable terminology to describe pleasure at work: a general sense of enjoyment at work; the ability to gracefully face setbacks and interact peacefully with colleagues, co-workers, clients, and customers; and believing that your work matters to yourself, your business, and beyond. With that criteria in mind, work-related happiness has been linked to nearly every desired outcome that individuals, workplaces, and organizations could wish for.

For example, happiness at work is linked to improved health and wellbeing, more creative and effective problem solving, increased productivity and innovation, and faster career development. People who are happier at work are more genuine, devoted, and motivated, as well as more willing to contribute beyond their job responsibilities; they also find more flow and meaning in their work.

People in happy workplaces tend to perceive the wider picture in the face of hardship and disappointments, making them less stressed, better at coping with and recovering from job stress, and better at reconciling conflict. They are perceived as more pleasant, trustworthy, deserving of respect and attention, and successful leaders by others; at happier workplaces, people are also more helpful and supportive of one another during difficult times.

Happier workplaces have lower turnover, cheaper healthcare costs, fewer mistakes and accidents, more efficiency, higher shareholder value, and a faster recovery from negative events or failures. They also earn stronger customer loyalty, commitment, and business growth through word-of-mouth referrals.

How can we cultivate, support, and create happiness at work now that we understand the nature and advantages of it? There is no common reply to this question. My purpose reflects my underlying values; and when my daily actions and decisions match those values, I feel more purposeful at work.

Although I am someone who longs for security and stability, I had decided to change from a good paying secure job to looking for employment again, simply because the values of the company were not in line with mine. I was demotivated and sad during my time there.

Bringing more passion and purpose to work as individuals can entail asserting ourselves in the formulation and execution of our daily activities, connecting what we do to what we believe in and care about rather than simply accepting the present status. If you respect equality and diversity, for example, you can make a point of working with people from different backgrounds. By providing on-site childcare and flexible return-to-work schedules for new parents, your company can instill core values of conservation and family into the workplace culture. If you have power, you can encourage purpose by making fundamental values explicit in the workplace and putting regulations in place that align people's daily experiences with core values.

Do you like your job in general? Are you a part of the decision-making process when it comes to what, when, and how you do things? How frequently do you lose track of time while working because you're intrigued or completely immersed? Do you believe you could be efficient and productive? According to research, most working people around the world reply no to questions like these, implying that workplace involvement is alarmingly low.

There are three major approaches to boosting workplace engagement. To begin with, incorporate laughter, imagination, and playfulness. Second, give individuals more control over their daily schedules, tasks, and professional development, and include learning and growth opportunities. Finally, create space for the immersive, lose-track-of-time sensation of flow at work by adopting a less restrictive, demanding timetable.

To achieve this, some businesses are moving away from the conventional hyper-busy, multitasking, always-available, gadget, meeting-crammed schedule while also encouraging off-work quiet. To help staff rest and heal, they are banning work-related communications after hours. The ability to cope, adapt to, and learn from setbacks, failures, and disappointments is essential for overall workplace happiness.

Resilience does not include avoiding problems, suffocating stress, or avoiding confrontation; rather, it entails being able to handle obstacles at work with honesty and humility. Getting better at real-time, in-the-moment awareness, or mindfulness is possibly the most promising strategy for increasing your own professional resilience. Mindfulness can be a beginning point for reversing our acquired patterns of self-criticism or blaming others or being fixated with past or future upsets, all of which make it difficult to manage challenging work situations.

Being authentic and bringing your complete and best self to work is another method to boost workplace resilience. The stress of surface acting or pretending to feel emotions you don't feel is eliminated when you are authentic to yourself at work. Workplace resilience is linked to the ability to disconnect from work successfully. This involves taking time off both daily and during vacations to recover and engage in restorative, non-work-related wellness, social, creative, and possibly charitable activities. Finally, you will be happier at work if you use your natural tendency for compassion to direct your thoughts, feelings, and actions toward meaningful social ties.

Treating others with dignity and respect at work entails expressing empathy and compassion, practicing gratitude, and constructively resolving problems. Building trust, sharing resources, feedback, and credit, and being a good listener are all examples of being courteous. I will further elaborate on the link between kindness and happiness.

Civility skills are essential for leaders to resist the corruptive influence of power. Practicing empathy, compassion, and gratitude at work is the next stage in being compassionate at work. We all want to be around people who have a positive attitude are happy . People are more imaginative and inspired when they are pleased. They are willing to develop their current talents and contribute to a fun and innovative workplace performance culture.

Finding happiness at work aids in the development of healthy interpersonal relationships at work and encourages employees to collaborate for the common good of the company they work for. It is the foundation of creativity, loyalty, accountability, and success. Happy business owners may foster a positive work environment that is easier for others to adapt to, and the more individuals that participate, the stronger the team becomes.

What happens if a workplace relationship breaks down? When forming part of a team I found that whenever I apologized, I created a trustworthy environment with satisfied colleagues. It took me years to realise that apologizing does not make you seem weak. Apologies generate greater respect and commitment from those around you and improve the ability of companies to recover from losses.

Here are the tips I followed to enhance my happiness at work:

- You don' t always have to wait for the team leaders to reward us. Give yourself motivation if you know that you have done your bit and given it your all. Small rewards boost work engagement, which is linked to perseverance, energy, passion, and pride.

- At work, happiness is choosing to avoid unpleasant thoughts, gossip, and hasty judgments. Happy people maintain their happiness by focusing on their deeds rather than allowing negative external influences to affect their feelings.

When apprehensive and focused, we are in a state of flow. It is defined as exhilarating, euphoric, and offering a deep sense of pleasure, and it involves skills and internal motivation. Flow is achieved through persistent focus, a high level of positive emotion, and the acquisition of new skills.

Exhilaration and mental refreshment can be enhanced by being creative with your workstation. It improves concentration and makes you feel excellent at work daily. Make sure you declutter your workspace.

A fifteen-minute daily fitness regimen energizes the body and eliminates the poisons that cause fatigue. Walking, jogging, cycling, swimming, or any other form of exercise is guaranteed to increase productivity at work, give you more energy to give it your all, and give you greater fulfillment throughout the day. This is particularly significant if you have a desk job.

Workplace happiness and job satisfaction are predicted by decisive and rapid feedback. Employers or supervisors that provide regular feedback and acknowledge efforts are more likely to have a happy workforce, according to studies. Make sure you participate when brainstorming activities are initiated at work and when asked to fill feedback questionnaires ensure you are honest and blunt about your thoughts.

When juggling multiple things at once, it's nearly impossible to give each one equal attention, resulting in distractions. We can avoid this by prioritizing our to-do list and concentrating on the most critical duties first.

Helping others brings us a level of happiness that cannot be compared to anything else in the world. It provides us a sense of authority, increases our knowledge, and helps us feel more connected to the company. Simple acts of kindness, statements of thanks, and extending assistance to co-workers in times of need can improve our self-esteem and make us happy at work.

Mindfulness, appreciation, and good communication should be practiced on a regular basis to reduce stress and aid staff in achieving their goals.

A small reminder to oneself, a tiny flashback to earlier accomplishments, can perform wonders in restoring happiness at work.

Take a few moments each morning to gather your thoughts and make plans for the day. Take a walk, drink a cup of hot coffee, and make a list of your daily goals. A day that gets off to a good start is more likely to be productive and fruitful.

The key to a pleasant work-life is effective communication. Happy professionals are always one step ahead when it comes to keeping and adhering to a flexible schedule. Long periods of time spent working without a break can tax the brain and bring us down, resulting in inefficiency and dissatisfaction.

CHALLENGE 2

List three work-related achievements you had at your present job. Choose some of your biggest achievements for this challenge:

If you have not awarded or praised yourself for these, make sure you do so now.

Boredom, disengagement, chronic stress, turnover, and even cynicism are prevalent today - a reality that my parents were all too familiar with. I believe in a different kind of work life. Happiness at work, like happiness in life, is a basic human ambition for the younger generation and thus the most appealing bonus a workplace can provide.

When hedonic pleasures such as positive encounters every day, appreciation, and job satisfaction are used to measure workplace happiness, the results can be fleeting. Happiness at work is more than a subjective emotion. It is the result of how we choose to control our thoughts, behaviors, and reactions daily rather than external forces like praise or rewards.

Think of things you would change to enhance your happiness at your present job. Examples would be more responsibility, better recognition from your line manager, less gossip, more flexible schedules, a less packed timetable, etc. Write them down.

_____

_____

_____

_____

_____

_____

Happiness in Relationships

When you're in a romantic relationship, it's critical that you both feel pleased and supported. It's crucial to remember that it's not your partner's or your relationship's obligation to keep you happy. Whether you're in a relationship or not, it's ultimately your obligation to look after your own happiness. True happiness comes from within, and it begins with you.

To get to where I am today, I learned to put my mental health first, check in with myself regularly, concentrate on self-love, and take time for myself to pursue the activities that make me the happiest.

I no longer assign people to make me happy: it is fully my responsibility. While it is ultimately your job to ensure your own happiness, it is equally critical to ensure that your relationship is a source of joy in your life. It's difficult to define happiness in a relationship.

Not only is each relationship unique, but each person within a relationship has their own definition of happiness. Some individuals define happiness as a life free of strife. For some, happiness is having a lot of fun, having a lot of romance, or having a lot of laughs. Whatever definition you use is closely related to your expectations, desires, wants, and requirements, all of which are subject to change over time.

Happiness is made up of two components: satisfaction and enjoyment; however, they should complement each other rather than compete. They have a distinct function to perform: neither is the foundation for true happiness more significant than the other. How well this balance of satisfaction and enjoyment works in your life determines happiness.

You've learned what true happiness feels like when you can acquire as much enjoyment from an activity as possible while still having fun! True happiness is when you are genuinely fulfilled in all elements of your life, and you are receiving as much satisfaction as possible while also fully enjoying yourself imaginable. It is a state that everyone should aspire for and attempt to attain. We join a relationship with the intention of being happy. Of course, who wants to be sad in the first place? We expect love to fill us with a special kind of delight that we've never experienced before. Love and relationships can be difficult and painful at times. However, no matter what difficulties we face, we can still find satisfaction inside our own relationships.

Here are some ways you can enhance happiness in your relationship

Always practice honesty! The best policy is always to be honest. Let your partner know if you're having a bad day in your relationship! Unfortunately, no one can read minds, so you can't expect your spouse to know exactly how you're feeling even if you think you're leaving the clearest signs. the majority of relationship issues stem from a lack of communication and honesty. Feeling misunderstood because of not articulating your feelings and needs might make you feel alone and make your partner feel inadequate.

To avoid these issues and build a happy relationship, you should be open and honest with your partner about both the positive and poor aspects of your relationship so that they are aware of how things are going. Being honest will make you feel more seen and heard in the relationship, and it will relieve your partner of the pressure of having to read your mind.

Do not beat around the bush! Many people use humor or sarcasm to express themselves because it helps to diffuse a situation or make honest conversation easier to digest. And while you may believe you are direct while sharing your feelings in this manner, you are not. Humor or oblique communication might lead to misunderstanding and misunderstandings, completely masking the fact that you're truthful! If you need to have a serious chat with your spouse, make sure you speak in a clear and direct manner, so they understand what you're trying to communicate.

This can be daunting at first, especially if you like to communicate through humor or other means, but the more you try being straightforward, the more natural it will feel. Being open and honest with your partner can guarantee that you and your partner are on the same page and can support one another, resulting in a better and healthier relationship.

Communication is key! Communication is an imperative component of every relationship and something that many couples struggle with. Effective communication, defined as expressing your emotions and needs to your spouse, can take a lot of time and practice. Setting aside time to "check in" with your partner in a serious way can help alleviate some of the worries of discussing your emotions with your partner, especially if you are not used to speaking these types of things. Committing to a judgment-free conversation time will allow you and your partner to discuss issues that have been bothering you so that you may address them as they arise. Prioritizing effective communication in your relationship will ensure that you both feel seen and understood, increasing your relationship satisfaction and pleasure! These types of check-ins also save feelings from festering and turning into major issues or arguments. While conflict is an inevitable component of any relationship, you can confess that you prefer not to quarrel with your spouses.

Utilize therapy if needs be! While it is ultimately your responsibility to achieve happiness for yourself, it never hurts to seek professional assistance from time to time. If you aren't used to doing so, it can be quite tough to practice self-care and self-love. Speaking with a therapist might help you learn different strategies for incorporating self-care into your daily routine. Other issues that may hinder your happiness on your own can be addressed by a therapist. To be happy, you may need to address previous traumas or emotional obstacles that are preventing you from being your best, happiest self.

Self-care on a regular basis and seeking expert treatment to identify the source of your sadness will make you a happier person, allowing you to find greater enjoyment in your relationships! Even if you are not currently unhappy, seeing a therapist to learn new strategies or have a professional someone to talk to about your feelings might be beneficial. Seeing a therapist will boost your emotional intelligence and your ability to find happiness in life.

Choose kindness! Everyone has terrible days, so no one can be pleasant all the time. Even though this isn't always achievable, being nice is a worthwhile objective. Kindness plays a crucial role in any relationship, whether romantic or platonic. Even on difficult days, focusing on being nice, regardless of your mood or whatever you're going through personally, will help keep happiness in your relationship. When your partner is having a poor day, this generosity should be extended to them as well. It's not simple to be gracious to your partner and yourself in every scenario but doing so will help you both be happy in your relationship.

Expect nothing! It's critical to be present in your relationships and being present can frequently imply contentment with the reality you're now experiencing. It entails letting go of expectations about how your relationship should be or how your partner should behave. You may never be able to find happiness if you cling to expectations rather than accepting your relationship for what it is. Rather than harboring unreasonable expectations about your spouse, your relationship, or even yourself, concentrate on living in the present now. This is particularly important for today's influence of social media. Couples post their romantic vacations and expensive gifts, leaving those that do not seem to meet such criteria disappointed and dissatisfied with their relationship. • Remember that not everything on social media is real and is not representative of the entire picture.

Take time to be with yourself! Taking time for oneself is an important aspect of self-care and, for that matter, happiness in a relationship. You do not have to do everything together just because you are in a relationship. Taking time away from your partner to check in with your emotions and refocus might be beneficial. It's crucial to spend alone time, even if you're an extrovert, to center yourself.

Yes, even if you don't feel like you require alone time, it is necessary. It's wonderful for you, but it's also good for your spouse, who, more than likely, needs some alone time to check in with themselves. Taking time apart doesn't have to mean not seeing each other for days or weeks; it can simply mean taking as much time as you need to practice mindfulness, read a book, or engage in a meditative activity. Prioritizing self-care and having some time apart can increase your happiness as well as your partner's, which will benefit your relationship.

Patient is a virtue! It's crucial to be patient and content with the existing state of circumstances in addition to letting go of expectations of yourself, your spouse, and your relationship. Stressing over where you want your relationship to go or how the future will appear will keep you from being happy right now. Learning the virtue of acceptance and being patient with how things grow in the relationship is a huge part of letting go of expectations. Don't hurry into a commitment if you're not ready and don't decide to move in together, get a puppy, or meet the parents just because you think it's the right thing to do.

Wait patiently until your relationship is ready for those types of milestones, keeping in mind that the "proper" time for each person and relationship is different; then enjoy your relationship as it is. While it's necessary to consider your partnership's future, you can't live your entire life in the present, so don't force your relationship into a position it's not ready. If you let it, your relationship will develop naturally, and you and your spouse will be happier as a result!

Be Grateful! No relationship is flawless, and it can be tempting to focus on all of the issues present in a relationship, no matter how minor. While it's vital to be aware of your relationship's growth prospects, it's also critical to center your contemplation on the positive side of your relationship rather than the negative. Finding something to be grateful for in your relationship, whether it's your partner's sense of humor, their support for you, or your shared interests will help you frame your relationship in a positive light, resulting in you being happy in your relationship and in your personal life.

Just have fun! It's easy to ignore the importance of having fun with your spouse! Relationships evolve through stages, and while things may appear to be all fun and games at first, couples frequently lose their sense of playfulness as the relationship grows. It's critical to keep a sense of humor in the relationship, no matter what stage it's at. Having fun together can entail doing something you both enjoy, such as playing board games, going on a date night, or doing anything else you both enjoy. If you're stuck for ideas, go back to the beginning of your relationship and reminisce the things that made you happy as a couple. Returning to these types of activities will almost certainly bring joy back into your relationship! However, you are not obligated to stick to what you know and are comfortable with! Exploring new things with your partner is also a lot of fun!

Do not be too stubborn! When you find yourself in a relationship that has been going on for a long time, you are bound to have conflicts. While this is normal, it is critical to move on from arguments once they occur. Holding on to little grievances or critiques will set you back in the long term and cause you to be unhappy in your relationship. You will be happier if you concentrate on not sweating the small stuff, moving past arguments, and focusing on forgiveness rather than contempt. While it is crucial to forgive and forget to be happy, it is also necessary to know what matters require further conversation. Ignoring problems and avoid talking about them to resolve them is not what is meant here.

Do not assign your happiness to your partner! It is critical to accept final responsibility for your happiness; this applies to everyone irrelevant of they are in a relationship or not. Happiness cannot be manufactured externally by your lover or through a relationship; it must originate from within. Expecting your partner to make you happy places a significant expectation on them, one they will almost certainly fail to meet, even if they try their hardest. If you are not working on this yourself to begin with, your spouse will not be able to make you happy or boost your happiness. Depending on your partner to make you happy will not provide you happiness but will instead add to your relationship's stress.

Show respect! Respect is the core bedrock and needs constant consideration before speaking or doing anything. It is expected that your spouse will follow the same rules as you. My official definition: respect involves putting the other person's comfort, wellbeing, and happiness on a par with your own.

Be loyal! When we know that someone is looking out for us, we feel relieved. When each partner focuses on always helping the other, relationships have the best chance of succeeding. If your partner has done something you believe is inappropriate or you don't approve of, discuss it discreetly rather than in front of others.

Make your relationship a priority! Let your partner know that the relationship you both committed to is a priority if you want to establish a stronger positive relationship. Spend time and effort talking about and addressing each other's desires and needs. Make sure you and your partner have some "quality time" together to reconnect and enjoy each other's company. Even though job, children, and other duties are all important, strike a balance so that your relationship does not suffer.

Do not fight over trivial things! When it comes to conflicts, strong and happy couples know when to bring them up and when to put them aside. If you can let go of something and move on and still enjoy your spouse, then do so! Bring it up if you can't seem to move on and are pondering or obsessing about anything. When you bring up an argument, make sure you do so calmly, privately, and at a convenient time for you two. Never bring something distressing to bed, and never while children, other family members, or friends are there.

Show affection to your partner! It is not enough to only feel love for someone; you must also demonstrate that love. Use sweet words, show physical affection, and leave little love notes throughout the house. Whether it's a verbal or material gesture, make sure you're letting your partner know that you love him or her. Remember that affection and kind gestures trigger happy hormones in your brain, so showing affection can benefit you, your partner, and the relationship.

Understand that relationships are hard work! A successful relationship recognizes the need to put in effort to keep things running effectively. That implies you may have to do things you don't want to do because they are important to your partner. Other times, it involves making an extra effort to calm down or listen to your partner's concerns, even if it isn't the most convenient or easy thing to do at the time. If you want a happy, successful, and long-lasting relationship, you must put in a lot of effort.

Make positiveness the focal point! Even the most amazing partners have less-than-stellar moments, and even the finest of relationships faces problems. Those desiring a happy relationship will battle the bad with the positive when circumstances are tough. If your friend is irritable after a long day, think about how much fun you had last weekend or how hilarious he or she was. If you've noticed that your partner, for example, is a tad messy and it doesn't seem to be changing, focus on the fact that he or she is a fantastic cook or father. Reframe your thoughts to remind yourself that your partner is wonderful and you are delighted to be together. The things affecting your happiness should not be ignored. Those issues need to be tackled too. But keep a positive mindset and do not get overwhelmed with negative characteristics only.

How to tell if you are happy in a relationship? Is it visible in their eyes, face, or laughter? Is it fair to assume that people in a relationship are happy when they don't fight or disagree with one another? We join a relationship with the intention of being happy. Of course, who wants to be sad in the first place?

We expect love to fill us with a special kind of delight that we've never experienced before. Love and relationships can be difficult and painful at times. However, no matter what difficulties we face, we can still find satisfaction inside our own relationships. To obtain true happiness in a relationship, we must first recognize and determine what it is. We must differentiate between artificial and true enjoyment.

Here are indicators that you are happy in your relationship:

- ☑ You feel content and fulfilled. You are no longer envious. In the present moment, you are certainly experiencing a true existence.

- ☑ You are not unhappy or weak because of the troubles and obstacles you confront in your relationship. They, on the other hand, make you stronger and more optimistic. You rejoice in those hardships because you understand that they exist solely to challenge your faith and this will help you in developing more patience.

- ☑ You are careless about the past because you have accepted it. You've accepted your partner exactly as he or she was. You've already forgiven those who have offended you, and you've also forgiven yourself.

- Your undying love for your companion has transformed you into a total lover. Your love is pure and you are fearless of not receiving love back. You don't waste time worrying about your chances of winning. You simply love unreservedly, which makes you joyful.

- You are unconcerned with receiving pricey gifts, dining in a good restaurant, or going around the world. Simply seeing your loved one's grin and realizing you are spending time together is enough to make you feel inexplicably happy.

- You don't keep track of what you provide your spouse and feel cheated if you think you're giving more than they are. Because your love is genuine, you may give them more than they deserve. Kindness is what happens when you offer someone more than they deserve. And knowing how appreciative you are, makes you feel truly pleased.

- Your relationship forbids you from injuring yourself. Instead, it nurtures you and aids in your development as a person. Relationships teach you how to look after yourself. It allows you to love your lover in the same way that you love yourself.

- You're not afraid to tell it how it is since you both value honesty in your relationship. You both appreciate and share honesty, resulting in an open and honest partnership.

- You don't feel forced to express your happiness in your relationship on social media or other public platforms. You simply enjoy your relationship in secret rather than trying to make others jealous or fuel your own vanity.

- You require a level of freedom that is both balanced and unrestricted. You're putting in a lot of effort to rid yourself of hatred, falsehoods, and other vices. You don't want to be enslaved by them. You, on the other hand, are content to be a slave to love, kindness, truth, and compassion. You know it's impossible to serve two masters, so you don't try.

- In a relationship, especially a marriage, physical intimacy is essential. However, it is not guaranteed to be always available. If you don't rely solely on physical intimacy in your relationship, you'll be truly satisfied. You feel that emotional, mental, and spiritual connections are all important components of a good and happy relationship.

☑ Grudges and bitterness do not exist in your heart. You are willing to overlook your partner's flaws and faults. You are pleased since you do not have a burdened heart.

☑ You're both not overly sensitive and reactive. You are free to state your emotions and share your thoughts with others. You pay attention to each other. You can have fruitful and amicable disagreements.

☑ You are an individual with an open heart and an approachable attitude. You do not keep your genuine feelings hidden. You can let your tears flow freely, whether they are tears of joy or tears of sorrow. You can maintain your identity as an honest genuine human being.

In a relationship, true happiness is more complex than we realize. It's more than just the laughs and celebrations we share with our loved ones. It can be found not just in happy times but also in difficult ones. When troubles arise in our relationships, we may feel sad and upset, but with true faith, love, and patience, we can still be happy knowing that those who consider re-evaluating your options if you are currently unhappy in your relationship. Are you making the best decision possible? If you've made the right decision, are you putting it into practice? Keep in mind that true happiness is a choice that we must make.

Do you feel happy in your current relationship/s? If you are not satisfied with your relationship, list the things that bother you.

_____

_____

_____

_____

_____

What do you feel is missing in your relationship/s?

_____

_____

_____

_____

_____

If you feel like you are satisfied with your relationship/s, list way you think you could improve them. Feel free to use the suggestions mentioned above.

_____

_____

_____

_____

List three tips mentioned above that you feel like you need to incorporate in your relationship/s and feel like these will ultimately bring happiness into your relationship.

List 3 things you notice that show you are happy in your relationship, from the ones mentioned above

🎯 CHALLENGE 3

Talk to your partner or friend (if you are unhappy with a particular friendship you value) and discuss ways how you can incorporate the things you feel are missing in your relationship. Write down if this helped you:

_____

_____

_____

_____

Happiness in Society as a Woman

If you ask any group of women about their lives these days, you'll almost certainly hear about how stressed they are. Marital troubles, parenting challenges, professional stress, and financial difficulties are all problems that women I know the experience.

Most of my friends appear to be overworked and miserable, and take medication. According to a recent series of research, women's happiness levels have been slowly declining over the last few decades, to the point that they currently report lower happiness levels than males, reversing the role from the 1970s. These findings have shocked some, given the socio-economic advances in women's lives over the previous decades; increased work possibilities, higher incomes, and more reproductive choice, to name a few.

Women who work outside the home, according to research, have the additional burden of caring for the house after work hours. Women are unhappy not because of the amount of work they do but because of the added pressure to maintain good social ties at home and at work. Despite working longer hours outside the home than previous generations, women are nevertheless expected to spend more time with their children than men.

In fact, today's mothers spend more time with their children than their mothers in the 1960s, when they supposedly were not asked, expected, or forced to work besides taking care of their children, family, and households.

Women have been persuaded to believe that they are in control of their emotional lives. They grow worried when they are unable to match expectations. The sentiments of failure that girls feel when they don't measure up to unrealistic cultural norms are the root of women's unhappiness. In our culture, girls and young women believe they must be good at everything to be wonderful caregivers, successful at the workplace and school, and attractive at the same time.

Women's expectations for success have risen dramatically in practically every aspect of their lives, including their job objectives, leadership responsibilities, and societal contributions. To meet such expectations, women are forced to sacrifice their free time and leisure. This may impart the notion that when a woman fails in one area of her life, she is a total failure. For example, where you come from, like many, you are expected to become a mother, and building a family with someone you love is the next big step in your life.

This may not apply to you, and because you have not managed to create a family of your own not made up of cute cats and dogs, society considers you a failure. Social connection and happiness are also very highly linked. Social connections have changed the definition for many lately, and these may only be based on social media, friends on your friend lists on social media, and your ideal followers.

This means that our happiness has become fragmented. Fragmented happiness refers to pleasurable situations in our lives that we get used to and take for granted. This leads to having our happiness fading away over time. To create a secure social network, women must put in a lot of effort. There aren't many other women in the neighborhood for mothers to mingle with at home, and women rarely have time to socialize at work. As women advance in their careers, they are more likely to work from home, further increasing their solitude. They are unhappy because they are lonely.

According to research, women may be more emotionally affected by social isolation than men. When women are upset, research shows that they reach for their children and seek support from other women, rather than responding in the "fight or flight" manner that men do. Being with other women has a relaxing impact, and women believe that their friendships provide them with additional benefits, like a calming feeling.

A drop in women's happiness could also be because women nowadays are comparing themselves not only to the woman next door but also to their male senior at the office. A comparison is easily made with social media networks and internet access. Measuring the cause of a changes in happiness levels in women is difficult because there are so many more things women are comparing themselves to today, as opposed to years ago.

Although the fact that improvements in women's lives have been made over the years, the increased burden and pressure imposed on women today cannot be overlooked. Women have increased social mobility, increased opportunities at work, increased freedom in their relationships, and more choices in general. Although gender wage gaps have been partly overcome, this is not always the case in every career or every country.

These luxuries, if you can refer to them as such when compared to previous privileges, leave women with increased expectations and stress. Women are progressively expecting more of themselves, for better or worse, to have families, work, nurture others, be competitive, and be skinny and attractive all at the same time. When girls are young, educational institutions should intervene to ensure that parents and educators give them enough free time to pick what is essential in their lives rather than pressuring them to be overachievers.

Girls and women would be happier with themselves if they were less concerned with being perfect. Schools must steer students away from self-reflection and toward more community involvement.

Research performed by the University of California found that young adults reported higher levels of happiness and mental wellbeing when they were more involved in their communities. Creating a positive circle and achieving a high sense of belonging is a determining factor in women's happiness.

Women of all ages, it is advised, should find opportunities to participate in common endeavors and build relationships with others. You will see individuals often if you have a regular meeting with others around anything from a book group to a babysitting pool; and before you know it, someone from one of these groups will become a long-term buddy. Especially for women, companionship is critical to happiness. Friendships become more important sources of life happiness for women than they are for men over time.

Here are some tips on how to heighten your levels of happiness in various aspects of life as a woman:

When taking care of a family, women are frequently held to higher standards than simply being responsible for the birth of children. Although there is currently a change and more men are staying at home to care for their children, women have traditionally been expected to either cease working or take several years off to raise children. For single mothers, the pressure is amplified by the fact that they must consider childcare issues as well as juggling an ever-increasing list of duties. Even stay-home mothers who do so for the first few years confront the problem of falling behind their male counterparts in terms of skills and experience.

If you are raising children with your partner, make sure you agree with who will stay at home or how responsibilities will be divided. If you are a single mother, make sure you avail yourself of whatever extra help you can, including childcare services close to you and siblings who over to look after your children while you are away. As a single mother, you are less likely to have your partner take the children out so you can relax for a day, so using such help can prove to be a great reliever. Raising children does not mean you have to isolate yourself from the rest of the world and miss the progress the world is going through. Make sure you form part of communities related to childcare or mother-related groups if this makes raising children easier.

If forming a family and raising your kids is not your next step in life, do not get discouraged. I used to compare myself to ladies the same age who have a place of their own, have a husband, and a child. Many, like me, imagine this is the ideal life. Their lives should be sorted out in this manner by the age of thirty. You must also be well advanced in your career. This is not the case for everyone. Without making any excuses, not everyone is the same and not everyone has access to the same education. Above all, my version of the ideal life is different from yours, and that is perfectly fine. This is not up for discussion and not an opinion. You may focus on learning how to play an instrument because you did not have this opportunity as a young teenager. Not having kids or have settled down by the age of thirty is not a sin.

Though some women's access to higher education has improved in recent years, several challenges remain. Although more women are pursuing postsecondary education, this trend is not uniform across races and ethnicities. Explore possibilities to continue your education if this is something you always wanted as a woman but never had such opportunities growing up. Look into joining groups in your local communities, ideally with the same interest as yours and look into government-funded schemes that can help you achieve the level of education you always hoped for. Some companies are willing to support their female workforce by sponsoring, funding, or supporting in other ways if they wish to study further. It is never too late to learn!

One of the most common mistakes that working women make is failing to ask for more. Females are paid less across the board, according to research, and many businesses will take advantage of this fact. Even if you start with small steps, it's critical to have this skill in your toolbox for establishing a fair deal. Asking for more does not only apply in the workplace but also in life in general. It is admissible to ask for help or out-source certain tasks that you seem to dread doing yourself.

Look beyond your physical appearance and stop comparing yourself to influencers on social media.

Create positive circles and make sure you involve yourself in communities that hold the same values as yours.

Work on the best edition of yourself without comparing your weight, height, and physique with that of other women, ESPECIALLY those on social media. Whatever you see on these platforms is merely a realistic reflection of their daily lives.

Of course, additional research is required before anyone can provide the ideal female prescription for happiness. Women may draw on what science has already shown to be keys to happiness for all people: spending more time appreciating our blessings, remaining connected with one another and our communities, and letting go of some of that idealism. After all, whether these studies truly depict women's fluctuating happiness, there's no harm in anyone, male or female, doing whatever it takes to find happiness.

◎ CHALLENGE 4

What is ONE thing you always wanted to do but never had the chance to do in the past?

_____

_____

_____

How would you plan to go about it if you had to do it NOW? Plan the time, energy, equipment, and money you need to do this. For example, if you intend to start piano lessons, you need a keyboard to start off with, probably a teacher, and some studying material like books, etc.

_____

_____

_____

_____

Do some research on how you can execute the above plan. This may include searching for an affordable keyboard or a second-hand one, looking for a teacher close to you, etc.

TIP: If you feel like you can go out and buy whatever you need and come up with the budget for this ONE thing, just do it. If you need more time because your goals require a little more work, do not worry. Keep this plan handy, and if something else comes to mind, list it.

List three things that are getting in the way of you starting this ONE thing.

For each obstacle you mentioned above, list one idea of how you can overcome this hurdle.

Happiness and your Health

Happiness instills in us a sense of optimism and a contagious cheerfulness. According to a recent study, people seek happiness in three ways: doing good for someone else, doing things they love, and doing things that are beneficial for them. Furthermore, the most upbeat individuals are the happiest in general. And the research doesn't end there: being pleased with your career, your closest connections, and taking care of yourself physically and emotionally are all linked to happiness.

Happiness instills in us a sense of optimism and a contagious cheerfulness. According to a recent study, people seek happiness in three ways: doing good for someone else, doing things they love, and doing things that are beneficial for them. Furthermore, the most upbeat individuals are the happiest in general. And the research doesn't end there: being pleased with your career, your closest connections, and taking care of yourself physically and emotionally are all linked to happiness.

Happiness is defined by most people as a sense of purpose and well-being. This cheerful mindset has several physical and mental health implications. This includes allowing one's thinking to be receptive to optimism. This generates optimism and vigor, both of which are important for a person's well-being. Happiness contributes to a person's ability to solve problems. A person with a positive mindset feels they can and desire to attain their objectives. Building physical, intellectual, and social resources, people who are happy are more likely to learn because they seek out other people who are happy.

Happiness lowers your risk of cardiovascular disease and blood pressure, as well as allowing you to sleep better. Happiness helps you stick to an improved diet and maintain well-maintained healthy body weight by means of regular exercise and through reduced stress. Being joyful encourages a variety of lifestyle choices that are beneficial to one's overall health. People who are happy adopt healthier diets that include more fruits, vegetables, and whole grains. Fruit and vegetable-rich diets have long been linked to a variety of health benefits, including a reduced risk of diabetes, stroke, and heart disease.

Regular physical exercise aids in the development of strong bones, the growth of energy levels, the reduction of body fat, and the reduction of blood pressure. Furthermore, being happier may improve sleep habits and practices, which are critical for attention, productivity, exercise performance, and weight management.

What do you consume in any given day? List your three meals: breakfast, lunch, and dinner. Jot down the snacks you consume during a typical day.

Breakfast

Lunch

Dinner

Snacks

◎ CHALLENGE 5

Is there anything you would like to be changed from the above, knowing what is healthy to consume and what will contribute to your overall happiness? Try implementing one change at a time. Do not expect yourself to change your eating regime overnight and be tolerant of yourself. If you did not manage to reach your goal today, know you will do better next time!

_____

_____

_____

_____

You can improve your well-being and overall happiness by practicing resilience. This means that rather than giving up, you learn from adversities and move forward. Creating a positive outlook on life can also help with your happiness. This means that you learn to see the positive sides of people and things. Though the two are related, optimism is distinct from positive emotion.

Rather than simply being joyful, optimists have a unique perspective on the world: when good things happen in their life, they give themselves credit, assign the cause to long-term attributes under their control, and regard each good thing as a sign of more good things to come. This lens through which individuals view the world enables them to maintain a greater sense of personal control over things, as well as health-promoting habits, and is linked to a variety of advantages, including longevity.

Increasing your attentiveness and becoming a better listener can make one more focused and positive. As I will discuss later in the book, generosity is a sense of well-being. Performing acts of kindness make yourself and others happy. If you are seeking to find happiness but are still slightly skeptical about whether happiness can REALLY affect your health, I will give you more reasons why you should choose happiness.

Another relationship between pleasure and heart health has been discovered by research. Heart rate variability is linked to cardiovascular disease risk. Increased levels of stress can cause physiologic changes in our hormones and blood pressure, in addition to being upsetting on a psychological level. The happier you are, the higher chance you have to lessen the effects of these changes in the body and increase your recovery rate. Your cortisol levels are affected by happiness, and high-stress levels may increase your level of cortisol.

If you have noticed a recent weight gain, disturbed sleep patterns, and elevated blood pressure, it may be because of increased stress levels. When confronted with a stressful scenario, happy people tend to create less cortisol, and this is what this workbook will help you achieve. Certain stressful situations in life may never be avoided completely, but you can choose how to deal with them. Levels of blood-clotting protein are also elevated with increased stress.

High blood clotting factors in the blood can result in thrombosis and hemorrhage, amongst many other health complications. Less happiness may result in increased aches and pains, especially in patients with known arthritis and chronic pain disorders like fibromyalgia. Arthritis is a prevalent illness characterized by joint inflammation and deterioration. It causes painful and stiff joints, and it usually gets worse as you get old.

According to research, having a higher level of positive well-being may help to minimize the pain and stiffness associated with the illness. It's possible that being cheerful reduces the pain.

Reducing my stress levels consequently reduced my cortisol levels, and this meant less acne breakout. I experimented with the journey of happiness; and after purchasing a home glucose monitor, I monitored my sugar levels. I exercised more and ate better as part of the self-care process. This was another reason for my cortisol levels to go down, thus reducing my previously elevated blood sugar levels. And like me, there are plenty of women out there who can vouch for these benefits of happiness.

Not simply shorter-term aches and pains, but also more serious, long-term conditions are linked to happiness. In the end, longevity may be the most important health indicator, and happiness plays a key role here. It's reasonable to assume that a happier you will also be healthier. A negative mood dissipates quickly in the presence of happy experiences. Strengths and qualities serve as a barrier against psychiatric conditions, and they may be the key to developing resilience.

The best therapists don't just repair damage; they also help clients recognize and develop their positive aspects. Positive psychology is a relatively young profession that studies the aspects that contribute to emotional resilience, happiness, and health, among other life-affirming themes. What we now know about these topics can help us all live better, more meaningful lives while also reducing stress.

A set of strengths - known as "mature defenses" - is another characteristic linked to good feeling and optimism. Altruism, the ability to defer gratification, future-mindedness, and humor are some of the attributes not shared by everyone and fluctuate across a lifetime. A healthy and conscious engagement with reality defines mature defenses. Even when the reality is not acknowledged, it is accepted. Rather than being pushed aside, uncomfortable feelings and thoughts are purposefully converted into less dangerous negative forms.

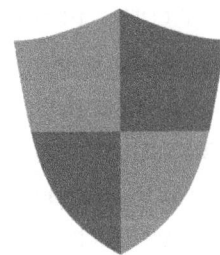

Unhappiness, sadness, worry, and stress are all connected to lower health outcomes, according to reliable evidence. Chronic exposure to these negative moods can lower immunity and promote inflammation in the body, leading to a variety of diseases and ailments. Positive psychology principles can help to overcome these negative emotions, boosting the likelihood of good health.

Being joyful may offer various advantages, such as lowering the risk of aging and stroke. However, further research is needed to back this up. To begin with, happiness promotes a healthy lifestyle. It may also help with reducing pain, the reduction of tension, the enhancement of your immune system, the protection of your heart, and the reduction of stress. Furthermore, it has the potential to lengthen your life. Although there is always room for more research, there's no reason you can't start prioritizing your happiness right now. Focusing on what makes you happy can not only make you happier, but it may also help you live longer.

Happiness and Money

Although you may opt to be wealthy right now, you may want to choose happiness instead. Although the media has persuaded many people that money equals happiness, this is not always the case. Money can surely assist you in achieving your objectives, providing for your future, and making life more fun, but it does not ensure happiness. If you don't understand how money influences your well-being, learning about interest or savings accounts is useless.

Rich people and countries are happier than impoverished people and countries, but the impact of money on happiness isn't as significant as you might assume. Increased disposable income has just a minor impact on your sense of well-being if you have clothes to wear, food, and a safe place to call home. Yes, money can buy happiness, but as you'll see, it's only part of the equation because happiness is our perception of events versus our expectations of life, money can play a role in this equation. And there's the real risk that more money may make you unhappy if your drive to spend rises along with it.

That isn't to imply that you must live like a saint. Finding a balance between having too little and too much is the key, and it's not a simple task. Money plays an essential role here, as anyone who lacks money can tell you. A better salary, for example, can provide safer housing, better health care, and nutrition, a more rewarding job, and more free time. However, this can become fully saturated easily. Once the fundamental necessities for food, healthcare, safety, and housing are addressed, the beneficial benefits of money, such as buying your ideal home are typically negated, such as working tedious hours or in more stressful environments, to preserve that income.

Our feelings about material purchases fade faster than our feelings about experiential purchases. Material items depreciate over time: the day after you purchase something, it is usually worth less than you paid for it. On the other hand, experiences are valued. Because you prefer to recall the positives and forget the negatives, your recollections of the activities you do, such as trips you take and concerts you attend, get fonder with time.

People are mostly motivated by their want to consume. The media instills a desire for the clothes and cars you see on television, as well as the watches and jewelry you see in magazine advertisements. However, research reveals that materialistic people are less happy than those who aren't. If your goal is to be happy, you must own and desire less.

Up to a degree, more spending does lead to increased fulfillment. However, overspending might have a negative impact on quality of life. Typically, as your income rises, so does your standard of living. You want to reward yourself when your boss gives you a raise, so you spend lavishly. It costs money to buy, store, and maintain all this new stuff. Your lifestyle gradually becomes more expensive, and you must work more to earn more. You believe that if you just got another raise, you'd have enough money. However, you'd very certainly repeat the loop by spending much more money.

People on the hedonic wheel believe if they simply had a little more money, they would be happy. When they have more money, though, they find something else they want. They can never have enough because they are never satisfied with what they have. We have been taught that wealth provides happiness, yet it turns out that money isn't everything. In simple terms, if you want more as you earn more, you'll never be satisfied, as there will always be something more you wish for, and you'll have to work even harder to have the money to get it.

You'll be caught circling the wheel like a mouse. The hedonic cycle leads to lifestyle inflation, which is just as damaging to your money as economic inflation; both depreciate currency. You have the option to opt-out, get off the treadmill, and get out of the rat race. To do so, you must first establish priorities and determine how much is enough.

Some people assume that if they just had a six-figure salary, their troubles would go away. Others play the lottery in hope of solving their challenges if they win. However, it is how much you spend in relation to your income that defines your happiness, not how much you earn. So, even if you get a pay-out, such as an inheritance, a bonus, or even a lottery prize, follow the advice of many thrifty millionaires and don't spend it all at once.

Knowing that you have enough can be more valuable than having billions. What good is money if you're obscenely wealthy yet unhappy? Enough is the key to happiness, not too little or too much.

Take some time to consider what it mean to have enough. Talk to your family about it and to your best friend. You're more likely to get entangled in the rat race if you don't have an end in sight. Because the concept of enough is so ambiguous, the simplest way to approach it is to be aware of your spending habits. Choosing how you spend mindfully can assist you in making purchases in keeping with your goals and values. Instead of spending impulsively, the aim is to spend with intention, determining where to direct your money.

Before making a purchase, ask yourself whether you feel like you will receive your money's worth. Make sure you contemplate values as opposed to purchases and make sure they are aligned. Make sure your purchases matter to you. Think of the clutter you have at home and whether you are constantly worrying about where to store things. If this is the case, you have surpassed the things you need to achieve fulfillment via material things, and you need to declutter.

These luxuries are not increasing your happiness but are making you more stressed. Getting rid of stuff is only painful for a short time. It's as if a weight has been eased from your shoulders once you've scaled back your belongings. You feel liberated. Some people find the process so empowering that they go even further and embrace voluntary simplification, even up to downsizing their living space. A fulfilled life is one that is well-balanced. To achieve balance, you must first determine how much is enough for you, or the point at which you are satisfied with what you have and can say, "This much, but no more."

Reaching this peak in your life means you have escaped the rat race, and freedom will prevail in your life. With less chaos in your life, you have more time and energy to spend with close family members and friends. Because external factors such as your financial situation play such a minor part in your overall happiness, it makes more sense to increase your happiness through a deliberate effort by controlling what you can and ignoring what you can't. Even though your economic status plays only a minor part in your total satisfaction, most individuals believe it is more significant. As a result, individuals spend their lives chasing after more money, only to discover that materialism makes them unhappy.

You may be dealing with credit card debt, living paycheck to paycheck, fighting with your spouse about money, and doing a job you despise if you're caught up in the rat race. All these issues arise from a single source: the loss of control. You're scared and stressed when you feel like you have no control over your finances.

Many of these tensions can be alleviated, and you can be happier by taking control of your finances. Wealth provides you with more options and allows you to focus on the things that will make you happy. You may acquire financial control over your life by living within your means and avoiding debt. Relationships, not dollars and cents, are the source of true riches. People with five or more close friends, whether wealthy or poor, are more likely to consider themselves as happy than those with less. This goes hand in hand with a long-term, loving relationship.

Spend your money on the things that bring you joy. It is not a loss to spend your money on things you will use and appreciate; after all, that's what money is for. You can afford items that make life easier and more fun if you spend less than you earn, satisfy your necessities, and save for the future. Anyone who has dealt with a long-term injury or sickness understands how emotionally and financially draining it can be.

Eat well, exercise often, and get enough rest. Don't measure yourself against others. Keeping up with others is a financial, psychological, and social trap. You'll always have acquaintances who are wealthy and have had more professional success. Concentrate on your own life and objectives. Mass and social media try to convince you that happiness is dependent on things you don't need or can't buy. According to studies, watching a lot of television might affect your materialism and how much you believe you need to be happy. Routine and consistent activities may increase contentment. So, sticking to a solid routine can help you remain happy; for example, try sticking to a morning routine: you get up at a regular time, exercise, meditate, have breakfast, and get ready for work, whether you are working from home or at the office.

If you enjoy jogging, schedule your runs and then accommodate the rest of your life around them. Don't neglect your responsibilities; instead, make the things you need to do fit around the things you want to accomplish, rather than the other way around. You'll save money and be happy if you simplify your life and reduce the quantity of stuff you own or aspire to own. The path to money is paved with ambitions, and the route to happiness is no different. However, for a goal to be worthwhile, it must be aligned with your beliefs and interests, and it must offer value to your life.

The bottom line is that no matter how much money you have, if you can't be content, you'll never be wealthy. Being satisfied is the key to good money management and happiness. It is how much you want rather than how much you have that determines whether you are happy or dissatisfied. You'll be content with less if you want less. The fewer your expectations, the easier it will be to meet them, and you will be happier. That isn't to say you should live a purposeless life of poverty; quite the contrary. However, most people mix up the means with the ends. They seek fulfillment through money and possessions, yet their decisions are impulsive and haphazard.

So, before you reach for your purse or commit to an order online, consider whether the purchase will truly bring you joy. Consider whether it will compromise your basic needs. Consider organizing a trip or enrolling in a class to acquire a new skill if you have some extra cash. Finally, remember that spending your money on others or donating it to reputable organizations may make you happier than spending it on yourself during this holiday season.

Do you believe that money can buy happiness? Why do you believe this? To what extent do you feel money affects your happiness? If you feel like money can affect your happiness, list three reasons why your happiness is dependent on your income?

If you do not feel like money has any effect on your happiness, list three reasons why your happiness does not depend on your income? Do you feel like you have everything you need?

◎ CHALLENGE 6

Let us play a little game. This should help you distinguish between the slight moments of happiness you get when you buy the latest phone as opposed to enjoying an experience that you will cherish forever.

Imagine you had all the money in the world, and you could buy three things, list them below ✎

List three experiences you will make you happy. To give you an idea, these could be going on vacation, going to a concert, attending a ceramics class because you always wanted to learn ceramics, etc. ✎

Now that you have listed the above, think of the happiness the latest phone will bring you as opposed to the memories you will have after attending a concert by your favorite artist. A few months down the line, a new model will be out, and you will probably want that too now. The memories, good time you spend with your friends, and photos you have created after the concert will not be overridden by anything. Doing will make you happier than having ✎

_____

_____

_____

_____

Happiness and Social-Media

While face-to-face contacts are linked to sentiments of fulfillment and contentment, many people equate social media with negative emotions. The most significant reason is social comparison. Viewing photographs and updates that selectively portray others positively may may cause social media users to underestimate how much others genuinely experience unpleasant emotions, leading them to believe that their own life with its mix of positive and negative emotions isn't as nice as others'.

Passive use, such as browsing through other people's posts and updates, entails little reciprocal connection between people while it provides plenty of opportunities for upward comparison. Fear of missing out, which occurs when you see people in your network having fun while you aren't there also contributes to unpleasant thoughts.

Humans are sociable creatures by nature. To prosper in life, we need others; and the strength of our bonds has a significant impact on our mental health and happiness. Being socially linked to people helps you cope with stress, worry, and depression, increase your self-esteem, bring comfort and happiness, prevent solitude, and help you live longer. On the other hand, lacking social relationships can put your mental and emotional health at risk. It's vital to remember that social media will never be able to replace face-to-face human interaction. To trigger the hormones that relieve stress and make you feel joyful, healthier, and more optimistic, you must interact with individuals in person. Spending excessive time on social media can make you feel lonely, as well as worsen anxiety and depression.

For years, I spent far too much time comparing myself to others, particularly on social media whether it was an old school classmate I barely knew or an influential person I'd never met. This act of comparison has been shown to undermine self-esteem by instilling the impression that there is always someone more attractive, skilled, or accomplished than you. This, I now realize, is not correct, but even a trace of it is enough to make anyone feel incompetent.

Inadequacy is a horrible sensation. You have a persistent demon on your back weighing you down in every aspect of your life. My confidence, on the other hand, received a much-needed boost once some social media networks were eliminated. Without continual exposure to everyone else's business, I've been able to let go of my feelings of inadequacy and replace them with the knowledge that we are all unique, wonderful, and deserving of a fantastic life. I've come to believe that knowing rather than revealing oneself on a social networking platform gives you confidence.

Without social media, I've learned to trust my instincts, cater to my uninfluenced wants, and seek only my own acceptance. My relatives and friends have made fun of me for not knowing what I want. The dream altered from day to day, the goalposts switched, and my progress became increasingly disconnected. I know that a decade of social media didn't help this and may have hampered my personal and professional success. I wasted time and energy focusing on what everyone else was doing that I didn't have time to focus on my own objectives and desires.

It's difficult to strive to be like everyone else all the time. It is only now, with a cleared head and no social influences, that I have begun to figure out aspirations and value accomplishments. This information is profound; it has inspired me to spend less time chasing other people's ambitions and more time pursuing my own. This can only be a good feeling for someone, particularly a woman. I'm no longer blindly following others on social media; instead, I'm starting to forge my own route and changing people's impressions of who I am. I hope that other women will feel inspired to do the same, whether they use social media.

Imagine having an extra month and a half per year to play with. The time that could be better spent getting in shape, reading a stack of unread books, or starting a new activity. Even today, women are frequently the homemakers and primary caregivers for their children, and they are expected to balance work and home life. We're always short on time, but we nevertheless feel the urge to indulge in things that make us truly happy. Those precious two hours per day spent on your phone add up quickly.

There was a time when I did things because I thought they would go over well on social media. It's easy to see why this brings us joy: the likes and comments make us feel respected and cherished as if we've accomplished something worthwhile. As a result, we may continue to engage in activities that we believe others will enjoy, sometimes at the expense of things that fulfill our own distinct goals. Furthermore, rather than being appreciated and recalled as an emotion, exceptional moments are sometimes spoiled in the chase of picture perfection.

Here are some tips to reduce social media usage if you feel like the applications on your phone have taken over your happiness:

Lessen the time spent on your phone by setting a timer for such apps to be switched off. Certain phones have a wellbeing app that monitors the time you spend on each app, and this can be a great eye-opener.

Avoid bringing your phone with you in bed.

Try disabling notifications for these apps, so you do not feel the urge to constantly check your phone.

Choose to spend more time with friends in real life by interacting with them on meetups, joining a club, or getting to know strangers.

Practice mindfulness or take up volunteering instead.

Don't get me wrong: some type of social media has a place in this world. It can bring friends and family together across massive distances, bring communities together for incredible causes, and give businesses a voice. However, there isn't much to like about it right now. Fake news, data privacy problems, trolling, and mental health difficulties have transformed what was once just a method for people to connect into a beast that is transforming how we interact with ourselves and others. It is time to re-evaluate your online habits and establish a better balance.

CHAPTER 3:
THE ACT OF KINDNESS

When was the last time a stranger treated you with kindness? Perhaps someone held a door open for you or offered you instructions on the street? We are all aware that being kind to others is beneficial. Kindness is a valuable attribute for maintaining connections and contributing to the development of a trusting and cooperative community. Perhaps you've heard that being kind makes you happier and healthier. What does this mean for you, though? What kinds of acts of kindness make us the happiest, and who benefits the most?

Being nice can make us feel better about ourselves or the significance of our lives, reinforce our self-competence, divert our attention away from our own problems and anxieties, provide a warm glow, or assist us in being more socially engaged. All these things have the potential to increase our well-being by lowering stress, enhancing mood, and offering community, and they may be more important at different periods of life. Helping others is a universal virtue and a very cost-effective strategy to help both others and us. Helping others is, as the cliché goes, helping oneself. One of the biggest advantages of kindness is that it spreads love in both directions; it's a win-win situation. I like to assume that the power of compassion will rub off on the individuals I'll be assisting in the future, making them more likely to help others.

As a result, science and studies demonstrate that being kind and helpful has a pleasant and uplifting influence on individuals who perform the deed. But, when you assist someone, what exactly happens in the body? The physical advantages of compassion can be felt in four different ways:

- Happiness hormones are released when you perform acts of kindness for others, raising serotonin, the neurotransmitter responsible for emotions of well-being and fulfillment. Endorphin levels rise as well, resulting in what is described as a 'helper's high.'

- Another physical advantage of kindness is that it can aid in the reduction of anxiety. Low positive affect, which refers to a person's experience of pleasant emotions like joy, interest, and alertness, is linked to social anxiety.

- Inflammation in the body has been related to a variety of health issues, including chronic pain, diabetes, obesity, and migraine headaches. Volunteering as a good gesture could help to lessen inflammation. Furthermore, oxytocin, which is also released after acts of kindness, decreases inflammation and has a direct impact on your heart's chemical equilibrium. Oxytocin induces the release of a molecule called nitric oxide, which causes blood vessels to dilate. Because oxytocin lowers blood pressure, it is regarded as a cardioprotective hormone, as it protects the heart by lowering blood pressure.

- Assisting others takes you out of your own head and can aids in the development of interpersonal relationships. Affiliative conduct refers to anything that helps you form ties with other individuals. Affiliative conduct appears to be an important part of coping with stress, suggesting that engaging in pro-social behavior could be a good way to reduce the impact of stress on emotional functioning. Furthermore, we experience feelings that can increase our immune system whenever we have an "affiliative connection" with someone, such as friendship, love, or other good bonding. As a result, it appears that ongoing altruism can improve your happiness as well as your relationships and connections, so indirectly improving your health.

So, knowing this, why aren't more individuals reaping the benefits of kindness? Why aren't more people making an attempt to make a difference in other people's lives? For one thing, generosity and compassion sometimes take second place in self-interest and vanities in our fast-paced world. People don't appear to pause to help others or even notice what's going on because we're typically preoccupied with our own lives.

Furthermore, some people believe that being nice and compassionate is a weakness that will only lead to them being exploited. But the truth is that it is in our human genes to be good to others. Kindness does not necessitate a lot of effort or a lot of time. It's something we can all aspire for daily. And, knowing that kindness has enormous power and rewards for both the giver and the receiver, why wouldn't you help others more?

On social media and in the news, we don't have to look far to uncover stories of generosity. Many of us appreciate hearing about people who help one another, strangers who are compassionate, and people who treat animals with kindness. These stories have a lot of attractiveness. If helping others benefits us as well, encouraging people to be nice could be a simple, low-cost, and effective way to improve happiness, wellbeing, and mental health.

Our bodies get saturated with the chemicals that make us happy and healthier when we perform just one act of kindness per day, which reduces stress, anxiety, and depression. Increased happiness leads to improved well-being, and what could be better than enhancing the well-being of one person? Improving the well-being of two persons. Not only does your body become overrun with hormones, but so does the body of the individual you're supporting. It's also contagious to see an act of kindness; it's a virus you want to get. Seeing someone conduct a good deed enhances the likelihood of that individual spreading compassion to others and infecting them with these habits.

Simple acts of kindness can spark a chain reaction, and all it takes is one person to get the ball rolling. It's important to remember that being kind doesn't cost anything. There is a strong correlation between gratitude and happiness. Counting one's fortunes can lead to a more positive outlook on life and positive thinking that comes naturally. By expressing your thanks through an act of kindness, you can practice both thankfulness and kindness. Although reflection is beneficial, expressing gratitude is where happiness thrives. So, send a quick text or leave a thank-you post-it sticky where your co-worker may see it. Offer to walk your friend's dog or make your best friend's favorite dinner for her birthday. You'll not just brighten someone else's day but also your own.

Performing small acts of kindness and showing appreciation and gratitude for what you already have will give you instant feelings of happiness. As I mentioned, volunteering with orphaned kids in southeast Asia has changed my life. For starters, I made sure I was emotionally ready for this. There are huge cultural differences, and you must take care of your mental health first before being able to help others. After the two weeks, I was able to appreciate having a warm meal three times a day, having accessible clean water every time I pleased, constant and good quality education, amongst other things.

If I complained about waiting in an emergency room for hours at my local hospital before, that meant nothing now that I know these kids could not get proper dental hygiene services or get their mandatory vaccinations as kids. Now, making my usual hot cup of coffee every morning is the time I start feeling grateful for what I have because as easy as this is for me, I know somewhere else in the world there are people who could not have half the things I have. This is the mindset that you need to adopt.

◎ CHALLENGE 7

If you are not in this place yet, try thinking of the things that give you the most pleasure. As an example, for me is the first sip of coffee in the morning and my ten-minute meditation routine. I do these things automatically without thinking about them. Use these simple everyday moments to remind yourself to be grateful.

And no, you do not have to wait for your new-years family dinner or thanksgiving dinner to go over the things you are grateful for in your life. If you have a romantic partner or a close friend, go over the things you are grateful for every time you go out for dinner, lunch, or coffee breaks.

This is your challenge for every morning from now on. Take something you do daily and make that your reminder for gratefulness. Use the journaling section later on in the book to keep track of these things.

JOURNALING SECTION

Performing acts of kindness can get you thinking about the way you want to be remembered. Think of how your friends and family will remember you after you pass away. If you want to be remembered for the good you did during your lifetime, you will easily find ways to perform acts of kindness every day. You may be thinking, volunteering across the world will require time off, money, and loads of planning. That is true, and you may not want to do this right now because you are not in a good financial or mental state, and that's perfectly fine. You can start small too. If you are a professor, you may want to dedicate some time after work to help kids coming from difficult homes do their homework once a week. These gestures do not require you to spend money. Time is money, and this statement could not be truer. By giving your time, you are giving money.

If you are running out of ideas on how to perform an act of kindness, here are some of my ultimate favorite acts, I can assure you that I felt instant gratification:

- Spend time with the elderly either at their houses or in an elderly home. A lot of elderly feel lonely because they have no family or have been neglected by their family members and end up lonely during visiting hours.

- Volunteer to help food banks distribute food to the needy.

- Donate food to poor people or homes.

- Help children complete their studies and homework regularly through private after-school lessons.

- Help in fundraising activities for a cause that has meaning to YOU.

- Gift small but meaning full presents during the holiday season to kids that will not be receiving gifts that year.

- Volunteer in an animal shelter.

- Donate food for animal shelters. Their needs are constantly growing, and the donations barely cover such expenses.

As you will notice, these giving ideas do not necessarily mean you will need to fork out money. Acts of kindness can include a skill, an activity, sharing a positive mentality or knowledge, be monetary, or simply giving your time. Feeling grateful can help you chose an act of kindness in line with your values so you can give to others and contribute to their happiness whilst enhancing your level of happiness too.

What are you grateful for? This can include a person in your life, a job, your health, and so on.

_____

_____

_____

_____

◎ CHALLENGE 8

Make a list of good deeds you think you can start doing more often to help others. List at least three.

_____

_____

_____

_____

Out of the three listed above, pick one in line with what you value more. As an example, if, as a woman, you feel like you should help other women in need, perhaps those who suffered physical or emotional abuse, you could volunteer your time, or money, or resources to help these women. The more in line with your values your act of kindness is, the more likely you are to stick to doing this activity regularly.

List things you know you need to perform this act of kindness; this could be anything from a sum of money to resources.

_____

_____

_____

_____

_____

_____

_____

_____

Make a commitment that you will perform this act X time a month. Make sure you schedule this into your monthly planner. If sharing it with others will help you keep you accountable, then share this on social media or tell your friends about it.

After you have done this act of kindness, come back to this workbook and write down how you felt afterward. You may use words like serene, peace, freedom, contentment, a sense of pride, etc.

TIP: When people know you are performing an act of kindness or doing something new in your life, they will ask about your progress as soon as you meet up, and this will help you share your happiness and help keep you on track.

CHAPTER 4:
TAKING CONTROL OF YOUR HAPPINESS

A lot of people are so used to feeling helpless, forgetting they are in control of their happiness; with the right mindset and skills, we can turn a permanent negative experience into a temporary one. This is something that has been taught to us over time throughout our childhood. For example, if you have failed big-time at your high school dance, you have probably given up on dancing in public. You now dread meeting your friends at the club because you are terrified of making a fool of yourself like that one time in high school. These experiences are some that remain with us for a long time and create a sense of phobia and anxiety.

There is always a reason for everything. The choices you have taken so far have always been driven by motivators or factors. For example, there is a reason you chose the house you live in, picked those subjects at school, and chose the car you have right now over the hundred other options available to you. These choices may have been affected by those around you. These choices leave no to little fulfillment in your life and are usually not exciting things.

Other choices were likely affected by what others told you to do. Growing up, I was always told to study medicine to become a doctor or pharmacist. Choosing anything else besides science subjects to study at school felt like I was betraying my family. These choices are more likely to increase your stress levels and will give you no gratification.

Remember, these are things your parents probably wanted you to study, not you. Other choices might have been influenced by the system and certain pre-requisites. You may wish to work with a particular company and be close by, but you move to a city you do not wish to live in. Maybe you'd rather live in the countryside, but because there is little job opportunity there or your commute will be longer, you are forced to move to the city. Finally, the choices everyone should be making are the ones chosen freely and willingly.

You are genuinely interested in the choices you make, and these choices will have you utilize your skills and talents. These are the ones that will leave you feeling accomplished, capable, and feeling powerful. You must take control of your life and make choices like this. Feeling more capable will give you more positivity, enjoyment, and fulfillment, contributing to your overall happiness.

What are the things you feel like you are good at? Try to identify the skills not listed in your resume / Curriculum Vitae that may not necessarily be related to your job. If you are struggling to fill this section, talk to a close friend or family member, and they will surely list some of your strengths.

_____

_____

_____

_____

What do you find yourself helping other people with? When do others come to you for help? Some examples of inspiration would be event planning, correcting schoolwork, and so on.

_____

_____

_____

_____

_____

What are the things you do every day that require you to utilize the skills you mentioned above?

_____

_____

_____

_____

_____

If you think that you do not utilize your skills enough, try listing activities you wish you could do more of. This does not necessarily have to be something you know you do so well. If you enjoy pottery, it does not mean you need to walk out of every class with the most beautiful vase, but it means that you are using the skills you have, perfecting them, and enjoying what you do.

What are the skills you use today at work that have helped you get to where you are today? As an example, if you are a human resources executive and you happen to have great people skills, then you know that you have utilized your strengths to become successful in life. This can also mean that your career gives you great satisfaction and you are in full control of your happiness.

Our happiness, like a million other things we are accountable for, is our responsibility, which is presumably why so many of us don't attempt! We are in charge of our careers, our health, our sleep, and our relationships, and on top of that, we must now figure out what makes us happy! It's much easier to point the finger at someone else. Happiness isn't a complicated feeling! Here's how you may reintroduce yourself with that feeling:

- The first step is to know that you are in charge of your own happiness. You are the source of your entire happiness. It is easier for you to feel happy the more you learn to tap into it yourself rather than relying on the mercy of others to do so. It will be difficult to keep up with your efforts unless you realize this. Every year, a considerable number of people commit suicide. Most of them do so because they forget that happiness is a choice, and they have the option of choosing happiness over suicide. I realize it's easier said than done.

- The simplest and most straightforward way to reclaim your joy is to begin to do things that make you happy. Humans have a predisposition for making simple things complicated. This is one of those instances. Doing things that bring us happiness puts us in a good mood, allowing us to focus on the rest of our tasks. I've personally witnessed the benefits of this. Instead of whining about how no one is available to go on a vacation with me, I now simply get a ticket and go by myself.

- The onetime I was halfway across the world in Southeast Asia, I tried getting people to stay for another week and visit another country in the continent after volunteering, but, understandably, a lot of people could not do it, either because of time off work, family, financial reasons, etc. But I figured that after a twelve-hour flight, I did not want to miss out on this experience, and I chose to travel to Vietnam as a solo female traveler. This was my first time ever traveling alone, in a country with so many cultural differences from what I am used to and a language that I did not understand.
Looking back now, I thank myself for being hard-headed and buying that one-way ticket to Vietnam, and not giving up on the idea just because no one could accompany me. I have been traveling the world solo ever since.

- As we grow older, we become more concerned with what others think of us and begin to act in ways that reflect that rather than living our lives according to our own desires. Your thoughts, not what others think, define the quality of your life, but we often overlook this.

As we grow older, we become more concerned with what others think of us and begin to act in ways that reflect that rather than living our lives according to our own desires. Your thoughts, not what others think, define the quality of your life, but we often overlook this.

You're doing two things when you complain: one, you're acting like a victim, and two, you're wasting more time locked in the past. I do not deny that you were treated unfairly by someone or anything, but the response to it is entirely up to you. Allowing what happened in the past to destroy the present moment is not a good idea. Play it back, make a list of the things you learned, and then move on. Complaining about it merely makes you relive that moment over and again while filling you with rage! Complaining about the past won't make a difference but improving the present by doing something modest in the future could drastically alter the future! People become so immersed in their own negativity and losses that they lose sight of the future they desire. Acknowledge the fact that you may have ended up being the victim in the past but do not sit there and feel sorry for yourself and hope others do too. What you make out of what is ahead of you is entirely up to you.

Choose joyous surroundings. You may be contemplating how you are going to do that. Think of the times you laugh during the day and how do you feel when you walk into your house or at work. Try to think about your feelings when you go out for a walk or meet friends. If your work environment feels toxic to you because you dread walking in there every day, then it is time to change jobs. If you hate your apartment, try finding something within your budget and your desired location that will give you more joy. If you hate that club so much and your next meet-up with friends will be there, let them know you do not enjoy it and you would rather go somewhere else.

One common thread connects the most vibrant locations and objects: colors that are vivid and brilliant! Colors put a smile on our faces, no matter how horrible the day is. If you don't believe me, consider how you feel when you see someone dressed in bright attire walking down the street. Have you ever paid attention to your reaction when you see a rainbow? I'm sure it brings you joy! Have you ever observed that most happy occasions necessitate the use of bright, vivid colors? Brazil's carnival, India's Holi festival, or China's New Year? During festivals across the world, vibrant colors are on show. So, create a vibrant environment for yourself!

Prepare to give yourself brutally honest critique, and don't forget to learn from your mistakes. What does anyone else's opinion mean if you've already examined and rectified your own flaws? Get to know your strengths and look for ways to put them to good use. You shouldn't be surprised by anything you hear in a formal appraisal or an informal statement. Don't count on others to point out your flaws.

You're asking for unhappiness if you compare your life to anything other than a previous version of yourself. There are different things you could be doing and doing so would require you to abandon your current route. If you continue your current route, you'll find yourself wandering around aimlessly, copying the latest success story you saw on social media. Make no comparisons to anyone but yourself. If you find yourself constantly scrolling on social media platforms hoping to become someone that you are not, it is time to clear those profiles.

Make sure you only follow people that inspire you to be the best version of yourself and not to compare yourself with them. Remember, what you see is not their entire life, but what they want their followers, like you, to see. Your decisions and the reality you experience will be someone else's vision of hell and vice versa. You must seek happiness based on your own definition of happiness, not someone else's. Certainly not based on television commercials, famous Instagram photos, or the lives of friends and relatives. Just because I do not have a family, a loving partner, and two kids to call my own, does it mean I am unhappy? NO! This is the ideal version of everyone my age, but it does not mean it is the happy version of everyone's life.

Before you ask for advice, work out your own strategy. Before you open yourself to accept suggestions, make sure you know what you want to do next. Recognize that whenever you reveal your objectives, you open yourself up to being influenced. Plan, stick to it and then share the outcomes, not the journey.

If you don't know what makes you happy, you'll be stuck trying to figure out how to get there. No number of social media or other people's opinions will be able to touch you if you can describe it precisely.

◎ CHALLENGE 9

Write down at what time you plan to wake up in the morning and what you intend to do right after. Try to incorporate a realistic morning routine that you are likely to stick to. If you have never run a marathon in your life, do not expect yourself to run 24 KM every morning.

Include the things you must do like go to work, buy your groceries, pick your kids from school, and going to that circuit class you always say you are going to go to. Leave time for your personal well-being like a skincare routine, showering, and getting ready for bed.

This is what this daily planner should look like:

01/01/2021

6:00 am- Wake up, make a cup of hot water with lemon, and stretch for 15 minutes.

6:30 am- Walk the dogs

7:00 am- Wake your kids up for school and get them ready if you have kids.

8:00 am- Start your commute to work and call the office on time

1:00pm- Lunch break

5:00 pm- Commute to your local gym and work out

6:30 pm- Stop at the grocery store to get groceries

7:30 pm -Prepare and eat dinner

8:30 pm- Read a book from your favorite genre

9:30 pm -Start your bedtime routine, whatever that means to you

DAILY PLANNER

_____

_____

_____

_____

_____

_____

_____

_____

_____

_____

Stop leaving your happiness in the hands of anyone else right now. Allow this to be a hint that you need to make a change if you don't feel like you're doing what you want to be doing or that you're not the person you want to be. There are people who take charge of their lives and those who are victims of life. Which would you choose to be? Which type do you think you are: the one who knows their own worth or the one who complains about being underrated?

No one can make you feel anything. Whether you're happy or sad, you have control over your emotions. Are you giving up control over your emotions? Make the call. Only you have the ability and desire to direct your own happiness. No outside influences should be allowed to enter your inner core. Nobody can force you to feel anything you don't want to feel; it's entirely up to you. You can do it!

CHAPTER 5:
CREATING A POSITIVE CIRCLE

Friendships shape who you are, what you value, and how you feel emotionally. If you discover that your social circle is not what you want, the first thing you must realize is that YOU have the power to change it. Those who have low self-esteem tend to associate with people who have little to offer. This makes them feel welcomed, if not a little superior. Expanding your social circle can help you live a better life. Helping you start down a more positive path, whether you're looking to expand your high-vibe mindset or culture more quality friendships, there are some steps you can take.

Creating a support system that embraces your happiness means you may need someone else's help, and you will find it, or simply means that sharing positive things with them is better than experiencing happiness alone. When you are fortunate enough to be around people who share your same values, beliefs, and likings, you will trigger dopamine to be released in the brain resulting in that feeling of happiness. Oxytocin will help with bonding with others. Spending your precious time with people that suck the happiness out of you, and make you feel like you do not fit it or seem like you are the weird one in the circle, then you are wasting your time.

This feeling is not permanent and may not even be real, you are probably in the wrong circle, and there are like-minded people ready to welcome you into their clique. Whether you match your community circle with sports, hobbies, religion, profession, geography, TV show, or book interests, make sure you are on the same page.

Think of your social circle and see if they represent the values, energy levels, and beliefs you have . If the circle you frequent does not share the same values, energy levels, and beliefs, I am going to give you ways to create a positive circle that matches your energy.

Friendships are beneficial to your health in addition to making you smile. According to research, having good friends in your 20s is a strong predictor of living to be 70, while having poor social support has the same mortality risk as smoking 15 cigarettes per day. It makes a difference with whom you spend your time.

Whether you want to strengthen your existing relationships or make additional high-value friends, attracting quality people begins with accepting responsibility for your actions and how they affect those around you and whom you attract.

The ideal people will naturally flock around you if you understand the qualities to nurture inside yourself. You attract what you are. If we want quality people to want to spend time with us, we must reciprocate with quality behavior. This entails assessing how we treat the people in our lives. No one is flawless, but if we expect others to treat us the same way, we should strive to create great behaviors. Because any relationship is only as good as the individuals in it, you'll want to focus on developing skills that help you form better bonds with others. This necessitates the development of interpersonal skills such as active listening, paying attention, respect, honesty, and tolerance.

Performing act of kindness, whether in the form of money, time, or knowledge, is a wonderful way to demonstrate that we care. Kind gestures should be made without expecting anything in return, but they will also motivate others to be kind and attract generous individuals into our life. Having a positive attitude has numerous proven benefits that not only make life easier but also attract quality people. Our approach has an impact on others around us. Negativity is naturally avoided by good individuals.

As a result, if you want to appeal to positive people, make sure you have a positive outlook as well. When you smile, the entire world smiles along with you. Aside from the numerous physiological benefits of smiling, such as stress reduction, blood pressure reduction, and the development of a stronger immune system, smiling also attracts more people and makes you more likable.

Simply smiling opens the door to meeting new people. You can't meet new, great people without putting yourself out there, even if it isn't always easy.

This may necessitate stepping outside of your comfort zone. Look for gatherings where you can meet others who have similar interests to you. Attend a workout class if you enjoy exercising. Check out the new art installation in town if you enjoy art. You'll have the opportunity to meet new individuals if you put yourself out there. Surround yourself with those who keep you inspired, uplift your mood, and support your ambitions. Let's imagine you've come up with a new company concept or a weight-loss objective. You'll want people to say things like, "That sounds incredible!" or "How can I assist?"

At the same time, as you focus on your new interests, you'll want to do the same for others around you. Even when we establish positive behaviors in ourselves, we might sometimes mix the good with the bad. Not everyone is deserving of our time. We can be brought down if we spend our time and energy on the wrong people. In that situation, we must learn when to move away from poisonous relationships.

You can't merely add great people to your circle; you also have to remove the negative ones. Cut relationships with anyone who isn't bringing you happiness, joy, or support.

You don't have to make a huge deal about it; simply cease giving them your time and energy, respectfully, of course, and note how much better you'll feel right away. Don't give in the next time one of your toxic friends wants to hang out or calls you to complain; instead, opt to focus your energy on someone else.

It's important to remember that being selective with your time and energy isn't selfish; it's healthy.

People who believe they have a lot to give the world will not accept a crowd that believes otherwise. You have to have faith in yourself before you can expect good people to want to be around you.

◎ CHALLENGE 10

Write down your qualities and what makes you a wonderful friend. Post your list somewhere you'll see it every day and remind yourself why you're wonderful every morning.

_____

_____

_____

_____

_____

_____

_____

_____

_____

TIP: Focusing on what you have to give people will help you develop a good attitude and boost your self-assurance. A room full of negative, weak acquaintances is less preferable to having a handful of supporting, nice friends. Concentrate your attention on the people who matter in your life and give them the time and attention they deserve.

CHALLENGE 11

Consume less time on social platforms this week and more face-to-face time with a friend whose presence makes your heart soar. Grab a coffee with them or invite them to take a walk outside.

TIP: In comparison to the unsocial world of social media, you'll be shocked at how valuable in-person friendships are. When it comes to extending your social community, start by looking for people you admire, whether for their great attributes, attitudes, achievements, or something else. Attracting these folks will help you adopt their excellent characteristics and attitudes.

CHALLENGE 12

Consider the persons in your life that you admire the most. Take note of their names and make an effort to interact with each of them this month, ideally in person. Remember to follow up and, hopefully, organize a second round.

_____

_____

_____

_____

Think of ways the people you mentioned above help you in the following ways:

_____

_____

_____

_____

How do they make you feel happy? ✍

Who encourages you to be the best rendition of yourself? How do they challenge you? Do they achieve this by comparing you to others or by putting you down? ✍

Who do you look for in the most difficult times? ✍

Are you able to turn to any of the people mentioned above, WHENEVER you need anything? ✍

_____

_____

_____

_____

💡 TIP: The more energy you invest in these people, the more your world will begin to transform.

We aren't all flawless, but we all have something useful to offer others. Your attitude will alter if you concentrate on what you have to offer. You'll raise your head a little higher; you'll start conversations; you'll be more confident. People react to these actions. You might even make friends with people you'd never consider hanging out with before. We've all met people who appear to have large circles of friends. They can strike up a discussion with anyone, anytime. We occasionally feel jealous of them.

Some people tend to focus on quantity or quality, but quality is the better option. When you have a smaller social community, but it is made up of people who understand true friendship, people who are there for you when you need them, and whom you can trust, you already have a fantastic social circle. It's not that your inner loop shouldn't widen; on the contrary, it should. Being selective, on the other hand, entails separating out acquaintances. We spend too much time hesitating when it comes to creating new relationships because we are afraid of rejection or inadequacy.

Get rid of your insecurities and self-doubt. Make it all about them in your approach. Ask questions, and then pay attention to the answers. Demonstrate real interest. People are usually receptive to such initiatives. We appreciate certain people for their accomplishments, general optimistic dispositions, or ability to get along with others. They also appear to have a network of good connections. These are the folks you should include in your network.

Get to know them better; this information will enable you to communicate with them on their level. You become more like people you admire when you can add them to your social circle.

Humans are social creatures; thus, we will naturally seek out other people to form relationships with. Relationships we seek and keep can either restrict or accelerate our personal and professional growth, depending on the psychological baggage we bring into adulthood.

Positive and healthy relationships are those that carry us forward. Identify those who can help you with this, seek their friendship, and see how much better your life will be. It takes time, patience, and devotion to building a positive community. Keep smiling, spreading joy, and putting yourself out there if it doesn't happen right away. Wake up every day as the best version of yourself, and you'll attract like-minded people.

◎ CHALLENGE 13

This challenge is for those who feel that they do not belong in their clique and need ways to create new bonds with people who will embrace their happiness, not hinder it. Let's say that you aspire to spend more time with a group of people you now occasionally frequent but feel like you belong with. You may be transitioning from the toxic circle you started with at the beginning of this workbook to wanting to create a positive circle.

Make a list of your skills and common interests you think you may have with the people you aspire to be with.

_____

_____

_____

_____

Bring up common interests in meet-ups, coffee dates, lunches, or walks in the parks. This can vary from that series you are all watching to the genre of books you all enjoy reading. If you want to meet these people on your own may prove to be a challenge, try taking a friend you trust along with you to help break the ice. If you are still seeking to find your clique, create one for yourself! Gather people you know would be interested in sharing a common interest and, most importantly, be happy together.

CHAPTER 6:
FINDING THE "HAPPY" IN EVERYTHING

Have you ever found yourself obsessing over a slight or obsessing about a screwup? Criticisms have a bigger impact than compliments, and negative news gets more attention than good news. Because negative episodes leave a stronger impact on our brains than pleasant occurrences, this is the case. This is referred to as negative bias by psychologists, and it can have a significant impact on your behavior, decisions, and even relationships. The negative bias refers to our propensity to not only notice but also focus on unfavorable stimuli. This is also known as positive-negative asymmetry, which suggests that we are more sensitive to the sting of criticism than to the happiness of praise.

This psychological phenomenon explains why terrible first impressions are so difficult to overcome and why prior traumas can persist for so long. We are more prone to notice unpleasant things in practically any contact and remember them more vividly later. Traumatic events are remembered more vividly than happy ones. Moreover, insults are remembered more vividly than appreciation. Negative stimuli elicit stronger reactions and more frequent thoughts in humans than positive stimuli. Negative experiences bring out a stronger reaction than equally pleasant circumstances.

For instance, you might be having a fantastic day at work when a colleague makes an offhanded remark that irritates you. You subsequently spend the rest of your workday stewing over his statements. When someone asks how your day went when you returned home from work, you express your disappointment and say it was terrible, even though it was actually fairly wonderful, notwithstanding that one negative experience.

This negative bias causes you to pay considerably more attention to the negative events that occur, giving them more importance than they deserve. People tend to fixate more on the bad when they try to make sense of reality, according to research throughout a wide range of psychological experiences.

We tend to pay more attention to negative experiences, and we base our decisions on these experiences. Unfortunately, people tend to learn more from the negative mishaps than the positive ones. It is the bad events that capture our attention more and influence most of our decisions. According to psychological experiments, the negative bias affects motivation to accomplish a task. When encouragement is portrayed as a way to get something, people are less motivated than when the same incentive is framed as a way to avoid losing something.

This can influence your desire to achieve a goal. Rather than focusing on what you'll get if you keep working toward a goal, you're more inclined to think about what you'll have to give up getting there. Furthermore, research has shown that people are more likely to believe bad news. Negative information may be perceived as having more legitimacy since it attracts more attention. I will help you overcome this part of your human instinct, but I would like to outline a few realistic examples on the matter. At work, you received a great performance assessment that emphasized your strong performance and accomplishments. You find yourself fixating on a few constructive comments that pointed out areas where you may improve. You're offended and irritated about the few critical comments rather than feeling good about the favorable portions of your review.

You and your significant other had a disagreement, and now you're fixated on all of your partner's defects.

Instead of focusing on their positive qualities, you obsess about their flaws. Even little flaws are exaggerated, while desirable features are neglected. Years ago, you embarrassed yourself in front of your friends, and you remember it well. Even though your buddies have probably forgotten about it, you find yourself quivering with embarrassment over it. Our proclivity to focus on negative events while overlooking positive ones is most likely a function of evolution.

Paying attention to harmful, dangerous, and negative threats in the world was actually a matter of life and death earlier in human history. Those who were more sensitive to danger and focused on the negative aspects of their environment were more likely to survive. Because of this, they were more prone to pass on genes that made them more alert to danger. According to evolutionary theory, the propensity to focus on the negative rather than the positive is simply one of the brain's attempts to keep us safe. According to research, this negativity bias appears as early as infancy. Positive facial expression and tone of voice are more important to very young newborns, but this begins to change as they approach one year of age. According to research, newborns' brain responses to unpleasant stimuli begin to increase around this period. This shows that a child's negative bias emerges in the second part of his or her first year. Some data suggests that the bias may begin even earlier in the development process.

Bad news, experiences, and information tend to impact our behaviors and attitudes more powerfully because negative information triggers a rise in activity in a major information processing area of the brain. While we no longer need to be on high alert all of the time like our forefathers did to survive, the negative bias still plays a significant influence on how our brains work. Negative bias has been demonstrated to have a wide range of implications on how people think, respond, and feel, according to research. Relationships, decision-making, and how you see people are just a few of the everyday areas where you could notice the effects of this bias. Your relationships may suffer as a result of your negativity bias.

People with prejudices may expect the worst from others, especially in tight interactions with people they have known for a long period. For example, you can have a negative expectation about how your spouse would react to something and enter the engagement with your barriers already up. Disputes and resentment are common outcomes.

When it comes to relationships, it is crucial to keep in mind that negative comments tend to carry a lot more weight than favorable ones. It's also crucial to be mindful of our own predisposition to dwell on the negative. You can focus on finding methods to give others a break and quit expecting the worst by acknowledging this natural human propensity.

The proclivity to overemphasize the bad has the potential to influence people's decisions and willingness to accept risks. When people consider scenarios involving either gaining or losing a given amount of money, the danger of loss tends to loom heavier in their imaginations. Even when the two options are equal, people typically fear the negative repercussions of a negative conclusion more than they desire the potential positive rewards.

People also tend to focus more on unfavorable information when developing impressions of others. When offered both "positive" and "negative" words to characterize another person's character, for example, researchers have shown that when creating a first impression, participants give the bad descriptors more weight. Negativity bias can have a negative impact on your mental health, causing you to obsess over dark ideas, harming your relationships with loved ones, and making it harder to keep a positive attitude in life.

Here are ways to overcome this negative bias brought down by our ancestors:

Begin to notice the types of thoughts that flow through your head. You can find yourself thinking things like "I shouldn't have done that" after an encounter. The way you think about yourself and others is shaped by your negative self-talk. Stopping those thoughts as soon as they start is a better strategy. Instead of dwelling on past errors that you can't change, think about what you've learned and how you can apply it in the future.

The way you talk to yourself about events, situations, and people has a big impact on how you interpret them. Look for ways to reframe situations in a more positive light if you find yourself interpreting things negatively or only focused on the negative aspects of a scenario. This does not suggest dismissing potential hazards; rather, it requires refocusing so that positive events are given fair and equal weight.

When you find yourself dwelling on problems, choose an upbeat activity to distract yourself from your bad thoughts. For example, if you find yourself ruminating on a negative incident or consequence, consciously try to divert your focus elsewhere and engage in a pleasurable activity. You can opt to go for a run or a walk, listen to some uplifting music, or reading a book you enjoy.

Because positive experiences take longer to be remembered, it's critical to pay additional attention to wonderful things that happen. Whereas negative events may be rapidly conveyed and kept in your long-term memory, positive events require more work to achieve the same effect. So, when something wonderful occurs, take a moment to truly appreciate it. Replay the scene in your mind multiple times, focusing on the great feelings it creates. A practical example of this is when something good happens in your life, and you quickly jump to the next big thing you plan to achieve instead of savoring the moment. You may feel uncomfortable accepting or acknowledging positive comments or compliments, when in fact, you should not.

Awe, savoring, appreciating, and capitalizing on pleasant feelings are all part of the positive attitude we want to apply more in our lives. Children are fantastic at noticing and relishing the pleasant things in life, and you need to rekindle your inner child. They perceive the good in things that we, as adults, take for granted. They allow themselves to be amazed, awed and inspired by anything, and they enjoy it. Our negative bias protects us, but it can also limit us from relishing and appreciating life's greatest pleasures as adults. A fresh way of thinking is required.

Give enough importance to anticipating something you are looking forward to as much as you give to actually doing it. This can be anything from grinding your coffee beans in the morning to brewing your favorite cup of coffee to planning that dream trip you have meant to take. Planning for your trip with your partner or group of friends should be pleasurable and can make you look forward to the holiday even more. So, do not just focus on pleasure once that things are done, but give enough attention to the anticipation of it as well. This can be done for the simplest tasks in life, like eating chocolate or seeing your high-school friend you have not met for a while. Having said this, it is important to not over anticipate or over-plan because mishaps happen, and you may be very disappointed or exhausted by the time you get to the experience.

What do you most look forward to during the day? REMEMBER that this can be as simple as making a fresh cup of loose leaf tea. Limit your answer to three things during a normal day.

_____

_____

_____

_____

_____

_____

Start planning your upcoming day the night before and put a star next to the activities you enjoy most. This will help you anticipate and experience happiness BEFORE doing the things you most love. So, just looking at your daily planner will bring you joy.

TIP: If you are struggling to find happiness in the little things in life, here's some advice for you, spice things up.

Suppose you enjoy coffee as much as I do: up to your coffee game a bit. I used to get pre-ground coffee and make my morning espresso in a stove-top coffee maker. This is until I learned that coffee, like any spice, loses its aroma after ten to fifteen days; and when my stovetop coffee maker began to get rusted, I realized that I needed to add more value to my day. I got a coffee grinder, which I can also use for spices. I invested in a coffee machine that warms milk and makes any coffee you can imagine. My morning routine now involves brewing fresh coffee beans and making a flavourful espresso. This is one of the things I most look forward to during the day. My coffee game has changed ever since; I am now the proud owner of a French press and coffee drip device. My morning coffee changes according to whatever I fancy on the day, and this cannot make me happier.

If you do not drink coffee, you can grow your own fresh herbs and brew fresh tea every morning instead. Get a nice teapot set and make the most of your morning tea. This will set you right up for the day with some excitement which you would otherwise miss out on. This can be applied for anything you do in the morning; if you meditate in the morning, get yourself an oil diffuser or an oil burner and fancy oils to set the mood. When enjoying your breakfast, lunch, or dinner, avoid working in the meantime. Enjoy your meal instead of rushing through the little relaxing time you should have during the day.

- ✅ Fuel these experiences. How many have you seen the perfect morning routine on social media, the one you follow every day and support endlessly. You probably have a morning routine of your own, and although you may not always remember to take a good photo of your morning toast, you should still enjoy the moment. Fuel your idea by sharing it with others, using social media if you like, or sharing it with close friends and family. These inspiring moments can boost your immune system and have an anti-inflammatory effect on your body. These will also help with anxiety, depression, and heart disease.

- ✅ How many of you look forward to their shower or bath at the end of the day? I know a lot of us do. Try to maximize your happiness in this area of your house. If you enjoy a warm bath, try to decorate the area, use candles or bath bombs if you wish.

- ✅ If you have a desk job, try to create a clean, clutter-free workspace that changes every once in a while. Change your stationery or desktop every once in a while.

- ✅ Look back at the positive times you lived, especially if you find yourself stuck in traffic or waiting to board a plane or a bus. Make sure you think of the bad times in good lessons, as I mentioned earlier.

What are some of your happiest moments?

_____

_____

_____

_____

_____

How do you feel when you reminisce these happy moments? Use words like confident, curious, successful, accomplished, peaceful, delighted, thrilled, and worthy, amongst others.

_____

_____

_____

_____

Although the negativity bias can have a strong influence on your behavior, being aware of it allows you to take steps toward a more positive mindset. One of the most effective strategies to overcome negative bias is to take a more attentive approach that has you aware of your own inclination toward negativity and consciously lifting brighter thoughts to the forefront of awareness. Because dwelling on the bad can have a detrimental impact on your mental health, taking actions to fight this bias can help you feel better.

CHAPTER 7: CHANGING YOUR PERSPECTIVE

Every day, we are all confronted with drama in many forms. It's not easy to maintain a cheerful attitude by changing your perspective. Someone is angry with you, things aren't going as planned, your kids aren't behaving, what's for dinner, why can't people communicate effectively, and you had a flat tire on your way to work. This may all happen in a single day! It's natural for people to think about themselves and what's going on around them, but this one-dimensional perspective can lead to a distorted sense of priorities. We can get greater insights and satisfaction by shifting our perspectives. If we want to be empathetic, balanced, and humane, we should change our perspective.

For many people, shifting perspectives entails becoming less self-centered and more empathetic toward others and the world around us. It is possible to phrase arguments in ways that motivate others rather than making them feel rejected, for example, by moving outside of our customary perspectives. Seeing things las "poor" without taking a new perspective might lead to a negative feedback loop. A breakup in a relationship, for example, might lead to poor thoughts about one's self-worth. A new perspective, on the other hand, maybe that becoming single marks the start of something new. You may even obtain a greater perspective of yourself as a result of reframing your perspective, embracing the part of yourself that may not have been free to express itself within the relationship.

You strive over and over to transform your life and achieve fulfillment, but something always happens to derail your plans. You believe it is simply not in the cards for you to enjoy your life after a setback, another setback. You can't handle it any longer. You have the impression that you are doomed to be unhappy. You don't even have time to work toward happiness by making positive adjustments in your life. Spending time on it would be inconsiderate because you have so much on your plate. We all go through difficult situations, but how we respond to them is entirely up to us. Even after realizing the value of perspective, there were still times when I allowed the bad to take over.

We will automatically acquire stronger levels of self-esteem and a healthier self-image if we express ourselves in a positive, appreciative, and kind manner. We can deal with judgment and defeat much better if we develop the practice of being cheerful. Not only does this new perspective strengthen our defenses against prospective adversity, but it also improves our problem-solving abilities. I thought of the following to help me return to a peaceful state of mind:

☑ To change your attitude and become happier, you must first understand what makes you sad. Make a list of what makes you feel bad or puts you in a poor mood. Keep track of this over the course of a few days. After that, go over what you've written. Recognize and confront your negative ideas. Only then will you be capable of transforming those negative thoughts into positive ones. Keep an eye for anything that is related to your job; for example, are you feeling unfulfilled, are you living paycheck to paycheck, and seem to have no control over your finances? Do you feel like you have a shortage of backing from family and close friends? Do you find yourself having no time to relax and to spend time with yourself, alone? Do you feel like you are old, and it is now too late to make any changes for the better?

Jot down the what is making you unhappy at the moment? ✍

_____

_____

_____

_____

List ways how you can change these things based on what you have learned from this book so far ✍

_____

_____

_____

_____

List one positive thing you can take from each negative thing you listed above. Making a list of your negative thoughts is a good first step since it makes you aware of what's going on in your head. Then you'll be able to recognize it, discover something positive to take away from it, and start your mindset change. You don't always know what you're saying or how it comes across to others. It is now the right time to focus on the positive. ✍

_____

_____

_____

_____

☑ When you're in a state of intense emotion, reasoning often takes a back seat. This can send you into a descending spiral of negative thinking. If the people with whom you spend the most time tend to be negative, it will be practically impossible for you to avoid being drawn into the same negativity. It's not only about the people in your life when it comes to managing the negativity you allow into your life. Consider the kind of content you consume and the messaging you enable to subconsciously program your mind on a daily basis. I have explained positive circles and communities, and this applies to changing your perspective too. Do your best to filter negativity from your life in every form.

☑ You must alter your emotional and mental inputs in order to alter your perspective. Look for positive influences in the form of books, blogs, and spiritual leaders. Don't simply rely on news sources that focus on the bad things that are happening in the world. Look for podcasts and news feeds that are committed to spreading the good news. You can even choose not to engage with people whose news feeds are full of negativity to affect what appears in your social media stream. Also, don't forget to use yourself as a source of good messages. Make use of affirmations and pay attention to your inner dialogue.

☑ Unmet expectations cause dissatisfaction. It's frustrating when we expect someone to accomplish something, and they don't follow through. We have no influence over what others do. We can, however, better control our own expectations. You haven't set somebody up for the best possible outcome if you expect someone who has shown himself or herself to be unreliable to follow through on something. To avoid drama in your life caused by unmet expectations, make sure you communicate expectations clearly and avoid forming assumptions.

☑ There is a lot of baggage in life we cannot change because we lack control over these things. Many of the daily dramas we confront, however, are just transient. You are no longer stuck in the horrendous traffic you were in earlier. You can choose to limit your time with a family member who constantly seems to find a way to say hateful things. The team member who is causing toxicity in your company should be given the opportunity to find happiness elsewhere. Although you can't change other people's behavior or attitudes, you can shift your viewpoint to see that the drama only lasts as long as you let it.

☑ As previously said, changing your perspective can lead to a plethora of beneficial outcomes and increased chances of pleasure. This is especially powerful if you alter your perception of your past. For example, you can argue that because of "the way you are," certain undesirable results are unavoidable. Others may have told you that you are aggressive or even hot-headed, and you may believe it if you concentrate on something in your life that you consider to be unpleasant and approach it from a different viewpoint, that you will feel better about it.

☑ We can become more empathetic to others by obtaining new viewpoints. However, it's critical not to revert to old negative thought patterns. A daily habit of positive affirmation of yourself and others might help you keep your perspective on the world in a better place than it might otherwise be.

☑ Seeing the big picture requires taking a step back and setting aside time to get the kind of perspective you'll need to be happy and compassionate. Avoid focusing all your attention and energy on that one negative thing is not the right approach. Take a holistic approach.

☑ Allow yourself some time to clear your mind, listen to the breeze in the trees, and slow down a little. Consider what matters most in your life, and, of course, the benefits of meditation can assist you in gaining insights into what matters most. You may change the trajectory of your life and find more joy by changing your viewpoint on it.

☑ Start Journaling! It's also known as a thankfulness journal. Others refer to it as a "positive journal." Whatever you choose to call it, as long as it's a positive title. It should be a reflection of you. The goal of journaling is to focus on the positive aspects of life. Examine what is working and what is not. When you've identified what's not working, think about how you can improve it. Because you're letting everything out, journaling can help you feel less stressed and anxious. It's pouring through you and onto the page. It's a relief.

After a long or particularly difficult day, you want catharsis. Get it out of your system as soon as possible. Don't cling to negative thoughts. You're trying to get rid of your grouchy expression and attitude. In your writing, always end on a positive note. Finish with a positive event, something you're grateful for, or something you're looking forward to.

As you concentrate on shifting your mental perspective from negative to positive, you want your notebook to become more positive. You may observe where your thoughts appear to travel instinctively as you journal more. It is possible that your subconscious is venturing to inform you that you need to make a change. Stick around for more tips for the perfect journal to enhance your happiness.

☑ Make a list of the things you should or could have made. Maybe you have meant to find a new place to stay or change your current job. Perhaps you had a job offer that sounded intriguing at the time, but you refused to go ahead at the time, but regret it now. List these things and jot down the reasons why you did not go ahead with them. The idea is to be able to identify the things that keep you from doing what you wish or want and what is holding you back.

☑ To help change your perspective, make sure you increase your endorphins. You can do so by exercising or going for a hike. If you do not have time for this or do not really fancy a fitness session right now, know that laughing, helping others, dancing, or walking outside, will also give you an endorphin rush. Get out of the cage you have created for yourself. Go out and discover those endorphins, whether it's through exercise or being in the company of others.

☑ There will always be stumbling blocks and roadblocks. Don't convert them into a prison from which you can't get out. It feels safe inside your shell. However, you are missing out on experiences. The future appears bleak. This is due to your box. Examine your journal to discover how far you've progressed. When you think about it, you'll see what you're capable of. How real are those boundaries and barriers? Have you put them on yourself as a result of something that occurred? It happened in the past. Is it still valid? No. You have no room for it in your life, therefore throw it out. You're a wise individual. You have a long list of triumphs to your credit. But you've encircled yourself in some way, most likely without recognizing it. Things appear to be less difficult when you have that rush of happiness. You have a sense of invincibility! The more you keep at it, the less difficult it will become. And before you know it, you've broken free from your comfort zone and are looking at life from a different angle.

I am writing from experience. I learned that the only thing I could change was my viewpoint and the way I approached everything. I concluded that there were two ways to look at my life: either I was destined to be punished forever and live a dreadful life full of suffering, or I was going through it because the Universe knew I was strong enough to handle it and that I would emerge stronger, better, and happier than if I didn't. The latter is my pick.

When I took the life-changing decision to shift my perspective, I felt relieved to know that everything I was going through had a reason, even if I didn't understand it. I felt at ease knowing that by simply shifting my perspective, I could instantly change my mood. According to one theory, it takes up to six happy ideas to counteract one bad thought. Because happiness is a state of mind, changing your attitude can have a significant impact on your own happiness. Indeed, "silver lining thinking" can help you see the positive side of things and reframe obstacles as challenges. If you can intentionally interrupt any negative ideas that may arise, you will be willing to keep the caring character you desire.

It takes practice to change your perspective in order to be happy. Consider such setbacks from a different angle. Recognize the value in your setbacks. Setbacks provide a wealth of information, fresh knowledge, and examples of what not to do. Determine what you want to do to be happy. Understand why you wish to modify your perspective. Then, in any order, try the resources listed above to assist you in finding happiness. Imagine waking up feeling revitalized and looking forward to a day filled with joy. Imagine going to bed with a smile on your face, knowing that you did everything you could that day to shift your viewpoint and have a good day. You'll have a better night's sleep now that you've done it. Take each day as it comes.

CHAPTER 8: CHOOSING HAPPINESS IN 10 STEPS

Do you ever have the impression that happiness is just around the corner? When you eventually lose weight, make more money, or meet a lover, for example? Do you realize you've fallen into thought patterns like concern or self-criticism that make it difficult for you to be fully satisfied with where you're at right now? Are you continuously having your mood invaded by people or things over which you have no control? Have you accomplished several of your own objectives and are now asking, "Is this it?" We humans, on the whole, are terrible at forecasting what will make us happy. As a result, we invest our time, energy, and money in activities that leave us feeling unsatisfied and wanting more.

Happiness is closer proximity to you than you think. Here I will be going over the ten simple and most effective ways of choosing happiness in your life. They do not have to be big changes done altogether. These can help you to live your best life.

(1) Start every day with a choice of happiness:

Is it possible to choose happiness? Yes! Many happy people understand that happiness is a choice and that it is up to them to make that choice every day. Others who are happy are not enslaved by their circumstances, and they do not seek satisfaction in people or things. They recognize that when we stop chasing the world's idea of happiness, we realize that the choice to be happy has always been right in front of us. However, simply understanding that happiness is a choice is insufficient. It still takes a conscious effort to choose happiness every day to fully experience it.

Rather than focusing on the negative parts of life, happy people opt to focus on the positive. They concentrate on specific reasons to be thankful. When they get the opportunity, they express it. And they rapidly learn that there is always something for which to be grateful. A beautiful smile is a lovely thing. But, more importantly, studies show that making an emotion-filled face has an impact on how the brain processes emotions. In the same way that our faces impact our brains, our brains influence our faces.

In other words, by choosing to smile, you can really train yourself to feel happy. Not to mention the smiles you'll get in exchange for flashing yours are certain. Positive thoughts, affirmative beliefs, and personal claims of truth are all part of affirmations. They're spoken in the first person and are in the present tense. Affirmations, when used on a daily basis, can help to relieve stress, boost confidence, and improve one's outlook. Affirmations should be carefully chosen, based on truth, and addressed to present needs for the greatest effectiveness. Here are assertions you can start with:

- ☑ I am a gift to the world and will not waste my precious time on sadness and self-pity.

- ☑ I know my brain and my heart will help me make the right decisions, and they will keep me safe.

- ☑ I matter to the world, and the world matters to me.

- ☑ The situation I am in right now will help teach me a new lesson.

- ☑ I let go of my temper and resentment to leave time, space, and energy to grow.

- ☑ I accept responsibility for my actions and forgive myself for the mistakes I made.

- ☑ am going to ask for help if I cannot make it alone.

- ☑ Giving up is not an option; I will persevere.

- ☑ The things I have been through make me who I am, a better person, than yesterday.

- ☑ I appreciate my family, my friends, and my colleagues because they are gifts.

- ☑ The people I choose to surround myself with are the ones that understand me and do not judge me.

- ☑ I am free to leave any situation if it is harming my inner peace.

- ☑ My work impacts the world, and I am beneficial to the world.

- ☑ I will let go of anything that feels draining to me.

- ☑ I am in complete charge of my future.

- ☑ I have dreams that I work towards every day.

- ☑ I believe in myself and know I am able to overcome any hurdle. I have the wisdom to do so.

- ☑ I am not comparing myself to others, only to the person I was yesterday.

- ☑ I am only striving to be the best version of myself and no one else's.

- ☑ All that I wish for will come to me when I am ready for it.

What do you feel is missing in your relationship/s?

_____

_____

_____

When will you be using these three the most during the day?

_____

_____

_____

Remind me to repeat these affirmations during the time of the day you picked above.

Use this space to create more affirmations of your own.

_____

_____

_____

_____

_____

_____

_____

_____

_____

2   Slow Down!

The majority of us have alarm clocks set to meet the demands of others: a child, a workplace, or a school. That is unlikely to shift in the near future. However, this does not imply that we must surrender control of our mornings in the process. Set an inspiring, meaningful morning habit by getting up a little earlier. Each day should begin on your terms. You will find ideas for a morning routine later on in the book. You can tailor these to your schedules and needs.

Being busy appears to be an unavoidable feature of modern life. We all have responsibilities, locations to visit, and other demands on our minds, energy, and freedom. It's difficult to put life on hold until you're ready to resume your journey! We agree that being busy is the default state for a full, satisfying, and important existence since it appears to be beyond our control. What would you say if I asked you how you feel when you're busy? Do you enjoy it, thrive on it, and require it in your life, or does it make you feel jittery, wired, tense, and even stressed or anxious? Perhaps you've seen indicators that you're overly preoccupied with yourself?

Our bodies and minds react when we have too much on our plates. Feeling anything from completely overwhelmed to the need for an extra cup of coffee is a clue that we need to slow down, check-in with ourselves, and take a break from our hectic schedule. If this sounds like you, keep these pointers in mind as you try to be less busy and find more time, space, and flexibility in your calendar.

Take these pointers as tips to declutter your schedules:

- ☑ There are duties in life that we are obliged to do, but there are also many we do not. This is your life, and what you do with it is mostly up to you. This applies to how you spend your money, energy, and, of course, time. Make the decision to postpone or cancel something you don't want to do. It is entirely up to you how busy you are and what you do to fill the gaps in your calendar.

- ☑ Priorities are the things that you give the most importance to. Decide what matters most and take care of it first; the rest can wait. Choose your priorities and honor them first, whether it's the tasks on your To-Do list, accepting an invitation, or doing nothing.

☑ It takes practice to say no. We do not do it because we fear of missing out, anger someone, or feel self-centered or guilty. Instead, consider it this way: saying no to one thing implies saying yes to another. Find methods to say yes to the things that are most important to you. It doesn't have to be a permanent no; it could only be a temporary no for today or this week.

☑ It's easy to think that being busy means we're important and that our lives are, therefore, meaningful and valuable. Holidays, invites, after-school activities, meetings, and consultations are how we assess our success. If we want to live a fulfilling life, we must have a full and varied schedule. An overloaded diary, on the other hand, frequently leads to an overworked body and mind. Because we're too busy keeping up with our hectic lives, we lose sight of the simple things that make up a happy existence. Being busy isn't a status symbol or a sign of success in life.

☑ Instead of thinking that being busy is a positive thing, consider the advantages of being less occupied. You may have more personal space, less stress and rushing, and more time to spend with your family and loved ones. Hobbies, self-care, and reconnecting with oneself and what truly matters are all priorities. Rather than attempting to catch up with life, catch up with yourself. Give yourself free time and try crossing something off your To-Do list or schedule for this month.

◎ CHALLENGE 14

Pick one activity you will refuse this month and briefly explain it below.

_____

_____

_____

_____

_____

What will you do instead? How will you use your NOW free time? ✍

_____

_____

_____

_____

_____

☑ Busy is different from productive. You can be busy and still not accomplish much. Focus on your priorities, stay away from distractions, work smarter, not harder, and get more done in less time.

☑ Warm baths and flowers aren't the only ways to pamper yourself. Self-care is everything you do to make yourself feel better. If switching off from gadgets, slowing down from rushing, listening to yourself instead of the world around you, and pausing the day for 10 minutes makes you feel better, then that is self-care in and of itself! Make time for yourself a regular component of your self-care regimen and notice how it changes your life.

What is a typical self-care routine you would consider for yourself? ✍

_____

_____

_____

_____

_____

Do you incorporate this routine into your daily routine? How so?

_____

_____

_____

_____

_____

If you do not, think of ways you could start doing that as from tomorrow. If you wish to start meditating and you are a morning person, try incorporating it into your morning routine. This may mean you need to wake up earlier than usual. If you wish, you could incorporate physical exercise in your daily routine because that is when you feel the happiest; start by enrolling in a gym or booking fitness classes. To encourage yourself to stay on track, make sure you keep yourself accountable for this and feel free to include a close friend or relative into your new self-care routine. They will either do it with you or ask you how it's going.

- Clutter is much more than the items in our houses, but it is a fantastic place to start. Consider how much time you spend cleaning, clearing, tidying, and categorizing. It's a terrific technique to make everything easier and faster if you have less stuff.

- When I'm thinking about one thing while doing another, I realize that I'm too busy. It's not so much about being busy as it is about feeling busy, and the best approach to overcome this is to be present and interested in what you're doing right now.

- Continuing from the previous point, multitasking may appear to be a nifty little superpower, but it actually makes us feel busy. We force our minds to focus on multiple things at once, causing our brains to become confused about what to focus on. Our brains must catch up when we go from one task to the next. Do only one item at a time if possible.

Life doesn't always allow for planning, but a little consideration can go a long way toward making us feel less rushed. We can see what has to be done, when it needs to be done, and what we'll need to do it. Less stress, fewer things we forget or overlook, and more opportunities to schedule much-needed downtime.

Stop trying to do everything by yourself. Make a plan for who cooks dinner and who does the dishes with the rest of your family. If your money allows, hire a maid and shop for food online to avoid the hassle of lines and parking. Pay your invoices using direct debit and use your phone to set reminders, so you don't have to rely on your memory.

Stop stuffing your diary to the brim, and instead of underestimating the time it will take, overestimate it. Allow yourself plenty of leeway in case things don't go as planned, and you could even discover you have extra time on your hands!

If you didn't do the washing for a week or two, I'm sure you'd have a pile that would take a long time to pick through. The same may be said for the dishes! It would only take minutes to sort if you did a little every day. Simple daily habits let life run smoothly with minimal effort on your part and divide large tasks down into smaller, more doable tasks.

Ask yourself the same question the next time you feel your life is becoming too hectic. Make a conscious decision to do a little less, choose a little less, and push a little less every day. You could discover that keeping your calendar simple provides you the breathing room you need to live your best life. When your schedule gets too hectic, it may feel like your life is being squeezed out. You have a lot of power over how busy you are.

3) Surrendering to be happy

Surrender does not imply giving up, abandoning power, or failing. It's not like waving a white flag of surrender. We've been so accustomed to striving and attempting to achieve a goal that anything that deviates from that formula feels like self-sabotage. Surrender is the peak of healthy and enlightened behavior. Surrender is the lovely, gentle state of acceptance. It's letting go of your goals, expectations, and judgments and allowing life to unfold and be what it is. It's that trust-infusing energy with arms outstretched. Relaxing and trusting that, despite the fact that things may not appear to be ideal or going according to plan, everything will work out in the end. This is how we live a life of true liberty.

We must be free of our limiting self-beliefs, emotional barriers, and negative self-talk, as well as whatever stands in the way of true growth and transformation. Finally, you will be prevented from living an incredible and infinite existence. The journey to surrender can be highly disruptive at first. You will doubt it, oppose it, and try to push things to happen, but when you totally let go, you will discover that surrender is the place where everything begins to move. Surrender permits us to enter our lives with an open heart, ready to receive, fully capable of manifesting, and willing to embrace the good, the bad, and the ugly.

Are you confident in your ability to move on quickly? Do you ever get fixated on how you thought a scenario should have gone? Take note if you have a habit of holding grudges or can't cope when things don't go as planned. In this case, you are the only one who suffers. Turning a nuisance into a crisis does nothing to improve or modify the situation. This may sound similar if you insist on doing more, going further, and pushing through even when it's time to take a break. This kind of conduct will leave you feeling stuck, lacking both creativity and fun! If you are a perfectionist or a control freak, this narrow-mindedness will prevent you from gaining new insights and distancing yourself from restricting beliefs. But I was certain that my approach was good. I've always been humorous and upbeat, but beneath that was a layer of effort, so regimented and controlled that I ended up doing nothing. I'm at a halt, obstructing my own progress.

Life had become unduly burdensome. Surrender was not even a notion I was familiar with years ago, let alone one I could imagine embracing. I had no notion I was about to start on a surrender journey. Sometimes you wonder if there is anything you can do to improve or leave a bad circumstance in your life. When the answer is a resounding no, the only option is to accept the situation. We often have little control over our circumstances, but we do have power over what we choose to do, think, and feel, and that is surrender. If you don't pay attention, you'll end up in flames.

Instead of arming yourself and getting ready to battle, take a deep breath and tell yourself to trust, and you'll find yourself safely in the arms of surrender. A more peaceful answer is required. When surrender knocks, we allow it in through awareness, personal growth, and intuition. It's a decision made in the present. Seeing reality for what it is and fully opening yourself to it. We are creatures of habit, and breaking habits is difficult. We may have to tumble down a few times before the message sinks in and we realize that the path we're on leads to nowhere.

It was not long before I had a couple of missteps before hearing the command to surrender. Wherever focus goes, energy flows. I'm still on board the surrendered ship. I don't think I'll ever stop learning, and I don't think you will either. I've learned that letting go when I don't want to is always best for me, so I'm quicker to answer to these situations. I understand that the life I genuinely desire is one that is infinite, free, and plentiful. If you are wondering what letting go and surrendering looks like: we finally let go of the limiting energy of control and force from that rich realm of surrender. We have entirely stepped out of our own path when we aren't in control. We're ready to receive, tap into the limitless possibilities that exist for us, and manifest a life free of limitations.

(4) Treat yourself with kindness!

Treating yourself with more compassion may not be an easy task for you if you often find yourself self-criticizing and low on self-kindness. There is a possibility for you to acquire the skill of being kind to yourself and learn to treat yourself with more compassion. Here is how:

- Leave time for yourself and do something that makes you happy. You can sketch, write in a journal, compose short stories, play an instrument, or do anything else you enjoy. Give yourself some "me time" every day to be kind to yourself.

- We are often ready to praise others' accomplishments but sluggish to recognize our own. That must come to an end. Make yourself aware of your accomplishments and give yourself credit. When you do something you're proud of, take a moment to reflect on it. Praise yourself and be proud of what you've accomplished. Give yourself a compliment.

Write some compliments you can give yourself below:

_____

_____

_____

_____

The inner critic is something we've all experienced. It's that tiny voice in our thoughts that is quick to judge and quick to criticize. Your inner advocate is another voice in your head: the one that defends you. When your inner critic mocks and scorns you, your inner advocate intervenes and makes arguments on your behalf. Your inner critic is against you, but your inner advocate is on your side. By strengthening your inner advocate, you can be compassionate towards yourself.

Maybe you did something you're not proud of in the past; maybe you didn't stand up for yourself and let someone else take advantage of you; maybe you missed a great opportunity because you were afraid; maybe you didn't follow through on a major objective. If you're furious with yourself, be gentle to yourself: stop blaming yourself, pledge to do better in the future, and forgive yourself.

Create a pledge you can return to every time you want to blame yourself.

_____

_____

_____

_____

Taking care of oneself is one of the most effective methods to show kindness. Get enough rest, consume plenty of fruits and vegetables, and exercise on a regular basis. Additionally, find a technique to de-stress, pamper yourself, and take care of your appearance.

What does self-care represent to you? Is it a warm bath, is it a healthy diet, is it a day at the spa? Make a list of these things and keep it for whenever you need ideas to pamper yourself. There will be no excuses like you do not know how to or have no idea what to do. This will be handy for whenever you need it, and if needs be, making a list of the things you need to make it happen. For example, if for me a warm relaxing bath is my thing, I know I will need scented candles, nice bath foam, and a bath bomb. I make sure to keep these things in stock whenever I need pampering.

💡 Taking care of oneself is one of the most effective methods to show kindness. Get enough rest, consume plenty of fruits and vegetables, and exercise on a regular basis. Additionally, find a technique to de-stress, pamper yourself, and take care of your appearance.

💡 Self-respect means appreciating yourself for whom you are rather than allowing others to define your worth. It's believing in yourself, thinking for yourself, having your own opinions, and making decisions for yourself. It also entails refusing to judge oneself against others. Finally, self-respect is about fulfilling your promises to yourself and doing what you say you're going to do. Maintain a high level of self-respect.

💡 I'm not a fan of retail therapy or materialism. However, if you see something you truly want, buy it. If it's pricey, save for the purchase. So not wait for it to come as a gift. It's your duty.

💡 Soothe yourself to be kind to yourself. Perform the following activities: Indulge in a relaxing soak in a hot tub. Add a few drops of fragrant bath oil. Giving oneself a scalp massage is a good idea. Rub your feet. Make a cup of hot cocoa with mini marshmallows and curl up with a mystery thriller. Turn on some music, lock the door to your room, and dance around in your underpants. After all, no one knows how to calm you down as you do. This is a great approach if you have a bad day at work or had an argument with a close friend or co-worker.

What can instantly turn your bad day into a better one? Is it your pet, your partner, or simply spending time on your own?

💡 You may not be an athlete, but you're a natural mathematician. You may have a melodramatic side, but you have a terrific sense of humor. Always remind yourself of your positive characteristics.

💡 You have two options when you fail, make a mistake, or do something wrong. You may either tear yourself down or build yourself up. The latter is the common option amongst those who are kind to themselves. Tell yourself that everything will be fine. Remind yourself of your former accomplishments to raise your morale. Then devise a strategy for dealing with the situation and put it into action.

Which options do you USUALLY choose? How can you change this now that you have already gathered a lot of knowledge on choosing happiness for yourself?

_____

_____

_____

_____

We all felt we were not smart enough or good-looking enough for this occasion, that man or this outfit. You should stop this negative talk and replace it with words of encouragement like: "I am worthy," "I am enough as it is," and " I deserve to be happy."

People who respect themselves honor their ambitions. They do not dismiss their dreams as frivolous fancies. Instead, they take their dreams seriously by converting them into objectives and devising a strategy for reaching them.

What are your dreams? Pick three realistic ones.

How can you achieve these dreams? Have you always wanted to work on ceramics and pottery? What do you need to get started? First of all, make a list of the things you need, including equipment, and start doing some research on classes you may be able to take in your area if you decide to make this dream a reality.

_____

_____

_____

_____

_____

_____

Recognizing your potential is a part of being compassionate to yourself. You should know what you want and go get it, as indicated in the previous point. Never be pleased with where you are or what you have accomplished thus far in life; on the other hand, it is being mean to yourself. Be kind to yourself by finding the balance between being content with whom you are and taking steps to improve.

Perfectionists are setting themselves up for failure. Perfection, after all, is unattainable. Is there anything nastier than making your own achievement impossible? Rather than setting a high bar for yourself, seek to improve one small step at a time.

Wanting the best for yourself is a part of being compassionate to yourself. And you must believe in yourself to achieve the finest results. Have confidence in yourself and your capabilities. Think highly of yourself.

Accept yourself in your current state. You have both strengths and faults. You succeed some of the time and fail some of the time. You're correct some of the time and wrong some of the time. Allow yourself to be completely yourself.

Be compassionate towards yourself. Think of someone you care and love and imagine what you would say to them. Think of how you would treat a close friend, if they were going through a rough patch. Think of ways you would reassure them and how you would make them feel cared for or loved for. Take this approach and apply it to yourself.

What would you say to a close friend who has confined in you because they are going through a tough time? Maybe they are feeling like they are not enough or feel unhappy?

_____

_____

_____

_____

There is only one person in the world with whom you will always have a relationship: yourself. As a result, you should begin to ensure that you are a decent companion to yourself. Being kind to yourself is going to help you live your best life.

(5) Think Happy!

There is an interesting distinction in how men and women process negative feedback. Both sexes are affected by the negative-positive asymmetry effect. The distinction, on the other hand, is usually found in how the emotions present themselves. Women are more inclined to internalize their emotions, such as sadness or depression, whereas men are more likely to externalize their emotions, such as outward rage. Much of our pessimistic thinking stems from the negativity bias, as I have described earlier. After all, being murdered by a tiger is irreversible, whereas losing out on berries isn't.

Your ancestor ensured his survival by assuming the worst from the rustling in the bush and fleeing, allowing him to carry on his genes. He'll be able to eat berries again another day. Having a negative bias is no longer vital for survival in our modern environment. Our minds, on the other hand, are still wired to be on the lookout for tigers or to be on the lookout for negativity. Negativity bias can become a severe hindrance to our happiness and quality of life if left uncontrolled. There are, fortunately, methods for dealing with negative bias.

Take time to reflect on your day; what are the highlights for you? It's the negative ones for most of us. Enjoyable, helpful events like smiling at a friend, completing a task, or learning something new frequently occur throughout the day, but they usually pass through the brain like water through a strainer, leaving a little imprint.

Meanwhile, stressful, often detrimental experiences like getting delayed in traffic and missing a meeting, feeling ignored by a friend or misunderstood by a spouse, or obsessing on anxieties or resentments, can cause long-term alterations in neuronal structure and function.

In fact, Mother Nature is stacked against long-term health and well-being in favor of basic survival. To level the playing field, we must lean toward genuine happy experiences and actively assist them in positively changing the brain. Here are ways you can overcome the negativity bias you have been handed down:

Recognizing that there is an issue is a solid first step toward resolving it. Knowing that you have a negative bias will assist you spot when you're lingering on the bad parts of a situation. If that's the case, convince yourself, "There isn't a leopard hiding behind the shrub." To keep me safe, I don't have to think about it."

When something good happens to you, make a point of pausing to appreciate it. Replay the event in your head a few times to ensure that the happy recollection is stored in your long-term memory.

List three positive events you would enjoy recalling because of the good feeling these give you; they simply make you happy.

Because of the negativity bias, the bad things you say or do to others will have a greater impact on them than the positive ones. If you punish your child, criticize an employee, or quarrel with your spouse, say or do five good things to keep your relationship healthy.

Simple pleasures should be sprinkled throughout your day. Although most individuals save up for big occasions like vacations, birthday parties, or huge purchases, large, infrequent events will not be able to counteract your brain's tendency to be negative. A better method is to spread out your basic joys throughout the day. Take a cup of flavored coffee out on the balcony every morning, read a novel for fifteen minutes every day, get fresh flowers for your desk and spend some time each day in a beautiful location. Little positivity things throughout the day can assist your brain in combating its natural pessimism.

Prepare a list of positive things to think of whenever your mind wanders to a negative recollection, such as wonderful memories, encouraging phrases, or lines from songs. This is something I do regularly. I've memorized a few of my favorite songs. Anytime I find myself ruminating on something terrible from the past, I start reciting one of them in my head. This quickly shifts my attention away from the unpleasant and gives me a boost in my mood.

List 5 of these positive things below:

Imagine a drop of black ink falling into a large container of clear water whenever something terrible happens to you, such as someone saying something hurtful to you. Although the ink appears to be very black at first, it quickly blends in with the rest of the water until it is completely gone, leaving just clear water.

Keeping a gratitude notebook is a good idea. Taking a few minutes every day to reflect and write down all the nice things that happened to you during the day can help your brain stay tuned in to all the good things in your life. By focusing on the positive, you may progressively rewire your brain to be happier. You will find a gratitude journal later in the book. I find it best to journal first thing in the morning. Between my morning coffee and gaining clarity for the day, I find journaling in the morning best because it sets the right mood for the day. Alternatively, you can journal for 5-minutes in the morning and then re-evaluate the day before you go to sleep to monitor whether your goals have been met.

Print up any emails you receive from people thanking you for something you did or from your employer complimenting you for a job well done and save them in your praise file. Keep anything in your file that proves how talented and intelligent you are. Then, when negative ideas are weighing you down, pull out your beloved file to remind yourself of all the good you accomplish. If you like to avoid using paper, store these in your inbox.

Maintain awareness of both a positive and negative emotion, with the positive emotion taking precedence. For example, experience joy while you engage in an enjoyable activity while also experiencing dread about a presentation you must give at work. Holding both a happy and negative emotion at the same time will help you remember that they are not mutually exclusive emotions.

Embrace a realistic sense of optimism. This entails telling yourself the most upbeat and empowering narrative about a situation without denying or downplaying the facts.

Suppressing or fighting unpleasant or stressful events only serves to exacerbate them. Allow them to be while you mindfully watch them with acceptance and self-compassion. Softly label them, such as "feeling hurt" or "desiring payback." This will assist the amygdala, the brain's alarm clock, to settle down and cease repeating negative experiences.

Breathe in such a way that your exhalations are equal to or longer than your inhalations, which will automatically boost the activity of your nervous system's soothing and centering parasympathetic branch. I shall explain further about breathing techniques later in the book. Recall occasions when you felt strong and capable and concentrate on those feelings.

Because the negativity bias narrows our field of attention, we must cultivate the practice of broadening consciousness to notice more of the positive aspects of our lives. We're surrounded by valuable information: someone smiled, a light turned on, a child giggled, and a flower grew. Even in the darkest circumstances, there are still hopeful, beautiful, interesting, and useful things to be found, even only in one's own mind's good intentions and values. Indeed, the positive feelings that accompany appreciating what is good assist us in facing, coping with, and recovering from adversity, loss, and trauma.

Be ready to gently notice what is happening when negative patterns begin to activate, and practice doing something, even if it is small, to break the cycle each time. If you tend to overanalyze aspects of discussions that you perceive are negative, find a pastime or habit that will keep you from overanalyzing, such as reading, going for a run, cleaning your house, or creating cheerful music playlist.

Take note of your negative self-talk and replace it with constructive methods. "You fool!" transforms into "I wish I had chosen differently, but I'll remember how I wish I had acted and apply it to similar situations in the future."

What are the least nice things you have said to yourself when you make decisions or do things you regret soon after?

_____

_____

_____

_____

List alternative ways you could say to yourself, similar to the example above.

_____

_____

_____

_____

_____

It's crucial to recognize how much control you have over whether negative words stick with you. Every day, we have numerous opportunities to soak up the good that is authentically offered in the next minute, minute after minute, and hardwire it into our beings. Knowing that you have this ability is itself a corrective to the brain's negative bias at a time when so many individuals feel reasonably helpless in the face of vast and unsettling social forces. It's also a fantastic tool for cultivating resilient well-being. By overcoming negativity bias and reprogramming your brain to focus on the positive rather than the negative, you can live your happiest.

(6) Find your direction towards happiness!

Finding the appropriate path in life is an existential challenge that we all encounter at some point in our lives. These steps can help you discover direction, whether you just finished school and trying to figure out your life, or you've realized that the life you're living no longer suits you.

While it is necessary to take time to consider major life decisions, over-thinking can lead to paralysis, delayed decisions, self-doubt, and, eventually, inaction. Ask yourself, "Is this a genuine issue, or am I using this as an excuse to not follow my passion because I'm afraid?" whenever an impediment arises. Finding the proper path in life is something you must do. This is not something that comes to you. You must stop thinking about acting and start doing it.

People are afraid, which is one of the key reasons they don't act. They're afraid of making a mistake, of things not working out, and of learning that what they believed was the "correct way" isn't truly right for them. You are free to change your mind at any time. Just because you act doesn't ensure you'll stick to it indefinitely. It's fine if it doesn't work out.

At the very least, you know that you need to try something else. Acting, living through catastrophic scenarios, and emerging with more knowledge and wisdom is far preferable to doing nothing at all. The question of whether we should trust our instincts is a recurring one, yet we must learn to trust ourselves. This is a learning curve that will help you better tune your gut instinct the next time. Start doing some self-research if you realize your current life path isn't serving your needs, but you're not sure what would. Observe when you feel the most alive, enthusiastic, and like you're making a difference in your daily life. Consider which hobbies provide a pleasant challenge and which make time seem to fly by. Once you have that list, develop a checklist that is like all of the activities.

Make a list of the things you enjoy doing the most. No limits and no specifications to be met; write whatever comes to mind.

_____

_____

_____

_____

_____

Individual strengths exist in everyone, although it might be difficult to recognize them. Because our abilities come naturally to us, we aren't often aware that a specific feature or talent that we take for granted isn't shared by everyone. Taking a strengths test will help you gain a better understanding of where your strengths lie, and some ideas for how you might use them to make a difference in the world.

Make a list of your strengths, whether they are related to your job or simply having life skills, like being a good listener, will do for this list.

_____

_____

_____

_____

_____

We all have individual strengths, and we all have a set of essential values that influence how we conduct our lives. We will be happy if we live our lives in accordance with our core principles. We won't necessarily make the best decisions about our life's direction if we aren't aware of what these values are.

Find a list of values and narrow down the top 10 and top three that resonate with you to determine which values are must-haves in your life. You'll be better equipped to make important decisions based on these values once you're aware of them.

_____

_____

_____

_____

_____

Finding the right path in life can be a rewarding challenge that requires a great deal of trial and error.

(7) Stop Self-sabotaging!

We've all witnessed our own self-sabotage at some point in our lives. We work towards a goal, and then, when we manage, we give up or turn our focus towards something else. Some people are more susceptible to self-sabotage than others, but we've all done it at some point and ended up shooting ourselves in the foot instead of shooting for the moon. Cheating while on a diet, avoiding work tasks, prolonging a more-than-necessary relationship breakup, self-medicating instead of facing issues, and so on. These behaviors can be so discreet that it can become dangerously difficult for us to recognize the pattern.

List the five self-sabotaging activities you find yourself doing.

I quickly mentioned the amygdala earlier because it was my intention to elaborate on it here further. Simply said, the amygdala protects you from predators, but it also causes anxiety, uncertainty, and insecurity by talking you out of your dreams and keeping you in your comfort zone. Paying too much attention to our brain's thoughts on our dreams and goals can lead to a fixed mindset and self-destructive behavior. Although humans rely on the amygdala for survival and reproduction, we must learn when and how to silence it and ignore its information as logical beings.

Your parents passed on a sense of love and happiness as a child. If you've learned that love is defined by yelling and insults, being in a relationship with too much peace and too many compliments could make you anxious.

Because of this, you might instinctively want to do something to self-sabotage happiness, so you can shift your concentration back down. Your negative brainwashing could also be the result of later-life trauma and challenges, which explains why you react the way you do.

What is a good way to learn from the past and thus gain relief from my suffering? List five positive lessons so you can start to forgive your past and move forward in a more positive direction. It is true that your past is now out of your control, and if you suffered child trauma, you probably did not have control even back then. But I am not here to help you pity yourself and make nothing out of the situation, but rather I am here to help you make the best out of the present situation and unleash your inner happiness, the same happiness you have been longing for and truly deserve.

Take the following approaches to stop self-sabotaging your happiness:

- Understand you are not your past behavior, and you are now an adult. You are responsible for your present life and what is to come.

- If you self-sabotage in a relationship, try spending time with happy and loving couples. Make an arrangement to meet them together with your partner frequently, like once a week. This way, their good ways will be transferred to you, and this can help alter the idea of happiness and self-sabotaging you received as a kid. This can help you redefine what real love and happiness mean to you.

- If you self-sabotage in your career, try spending time with successful people and apply their strategy to your corporate world.

- Find comfort in talking about your repressed feelings with family members you trust or close friends. You will have less trouble dealing with your subconscious and will be less likely to self-sabotage your happiness.

- Recognize that there are things that trigger your past traumas, and that is perfectly understandable. Try to eliminate as many of these as possible. Replace these with things that remind you of happiness instead. For example, if the loss of a parent triggers unhappiness in you for obvious reasons, try replacing their personal belongings around the house with more lively and optimistic options like flowers or colorful furniture decorations.

- Make sure there is meaning in your life. Without meaning, you are more likely to self-sabotage and look for negative attributes to focus on, and that is not what you want. Try devoting most of your time to a hobby or long-awaited passions. Take on some exciting projects, redecorating, or remodeling a room in your house. For me, this would be reading. Between the pandemic and other life situations, I found comfort in reading. I was blessed to find someone who shared the love I have for books as much as I do. Now, we buy and exchange books and talk about these when one of us has finished a book. We also keep each other accountable and ask about the progress we made on our yearly reading challenge. Today, we meet for coffee dates and read together or talk about stories we read in our last book.

What is the next project you want to be passionate about? This can be anything: cycling, painting, scuba diving, and so on.

_____

_____

_____

Your inner critic is that voice that exists solely to persuade you that you are a failure. If you've attempted to ignore it before, you know it's far easier said than done. Instead of dismissing your inner critic, become intrigued about what it is trying to teach you. What kind of apprehension is it reflecting onto the situation? What does the rest of you have to say about it? Because no decision is made alone, why not switch from monologues to the conversation? Allow each voice in your head to speak for a few moments. Do not just listen and do as your inner critic says, listening to this voice allows you to evaluate the situations and the different outcomes, not succumb to them as you have done in the past.

It's easier to take a painful certainty than to take a chance on the unknown. If you're unhappy with your current position, no amount of thankfulness or affirmations will help until you take steps to improve it. If you're still justifying not following your aspirations as "practical" or believing "things aren't that awful," keep in mind that most people only act when the agony of their current position outweighs their dread of the unknown. You may either wait until you reach rock bottom or jump right to the phase where you accept change. It's not sustainable if you're not pleased. Something will have to change eventually, and that is your next move.

Determine the limiting notion that is keeping you from acting. Then act. "What would someone who isn't afraid do?" you might wonder. Recognize your uneasiness and act anyway. Building a track record will help you overcome your fears, making it easier to act toward your goals.

The fear of failure stems from a wish to feel secure. The issue is that it also holds us in a state of stagnation. We often forget that making a mistake is different from being a "failure." To put it another way, it's just a useful, albeit unpleasant, learning experience. And if you think you're the only one who's ever failed, just look at any artist or entrepreneur, and you'll see that you're not alone.

Sure, you've slipped. There are plenty of them. Hopefully, you took something away from them. However, if you're still holding on to your grief and shame rather than surrendering and forgiving yourself, compassion may be in order. It's difficult and unpleasant, but it's the first step toward letting go of your old tale and beginning a new one. Allow it to go. You'll never be able to go forward if you keep berating yourself. Because you won't be able to change the past, concentrate on whom you want to be and what you want to achieve in the future.

That strong desire for control kept me secure, but it also kept me trapped. Surrendering goals taught me that letting go of what I want makes room for greater and better things to enter my life. You may be hindering yourself from meeting someone who is right for you if you try to control your relationship rather than understanding it's time to end things. Trying to control things prevents you from developing and accepting yourself. Change what you can, relinquish what you can't, and understand the difference.

If you leave your happiness at the mercy of others, you'll never be able to give it to yourself. Your connections with others should reflect your personal happiness and affection. It's not selfish to put yourself first. You are to blame if you've ever put people first and subsequently disliked them for it. Setting a boundary may seem harsh, but it is sometimes the best way to avoid an emotional aftertaste. It's time to stop longing to be saved and start saving yourself. Perhaps it's time to work more, make new relationships, or take care of your own needs. If you're new at setting limits, focus on minor details rather than your core principles.

It may be time to re-evaluate your responsibilities if your social life is more draining than fun. You are more likely to burnout if you don't make time for yourself. You may be settling for acquaintance rather than true friendship if you spend time with someone you don't really enjoy.

An hour on the treadmill is less physically and emotionally draining than an hour with a negative person. Think of where you want to put your energy. Do you still feel compelled to fulfill a promise? Consider what someone with self-compassion might do in this situation.

Everything I blamed on others was my fault, and everything I blamed on myself was the fault of someone else. You have the power to change the present, regardless of who is at fault or who accepts responsibility. It's easy to fall into the "I wish things were better" trap, but it just serves to keep you trapped. Take responsibility for what you want to create, not just for what happened. Self-awareness empowers you to assume personal responsibility with courage and humility.

You still would not be happy if you had the power to change others because it's more about feeling protected than it is about fixing. Accept them as they are, not as you wish they were. Change the one thing you have power over yourself. That requires adjusting or letting go of your expectations.

It's fantastic to give it your all, but if your happiness is dependent on the outcome, you'll be disappointed. Nothing in this world is flawless. Perfectionism is frequently what prevents us from taking the first step or being satisfied with the product. You want to take over the world, but if you're killing yourself in the process, it's possible that you're accomplishing to feel validated and worthy.

Realize that the comparison is a tool to tell you what you want in life. Inspiration is the healthy by-product of jealousy. If you're overly focused on what you don't have, you'll never notice all the great things own. Comparison should only be made with yourself. Aim to get happier, healthier, and stronger than you were the day before.

Most people decide how they're performing by consciously or unconsciously obtaining feedback from others. And, because you're hardwired to strive to impress others, you're more likely to try to please individuals who aren't easily moved. The opinions of others are not more important than your own. It makes no difference whether they are older, more successful, or more educated. Their point of view is just that: a point of view. Regardless of who disagrees, decide what is best for you.

Nobody has all the answers. Most individuals simply pretend it. Most of us avoid being vulnerable at all costs in a world that fosters self-sufficiency. Whether it's a desire to appear perfect, a fear of abandonment, or the urge to be liked, it's a manifestation of fear. Just be certain you're asking the proper people when asking for help, and no it is not a sign of weakness. Although convenient, your partner, friends, and parents aren't always the ideal sources.

Self-sabotage is a continuous process. It's a methodical procedure. Nobody is content all the time. However, if you sabotage your best efforts by judging yourself, evading responsibility, or exerting control over others, you will remain in this situation indefinitely. Happiness isn't merely a state of mind. It's a way of life and a decision.

⑧ Think Positivity!

Setting optimistic expectations in this environment of negativity is critical for developing a good and productive attitude in all situations. The first step toward real-life success is to set high expectations for yourself. If you are suffering from failures in your life, you must overcome negative beliefs; yet you must never assume that you are incapable of completing a task.

Fear is something that prevents us from trying new things, even though we may not be capable of doing so. If you want to do anything big, the first step is to overcome your fear and gain the confidence to begin doing what you desire. Try to cope with the situation fearlessly so that you can view the bright side of things with a constructive eye. You may live a remarkable life by removing fear from your life, and you will undoubtedly succeed in all areas of life.

The more optimistic expectations you give a space in your head, the better things and chances will come your way.

Such a positive view on life draws a lot of good things since optimism attracts a lot of positive qualities that make you a great person, among other things. Positive energy and excellent opportunities will eventually make their way to you, assisting you in becoming a successful person in life. This is what lately is being referred to as manifesting. You bring to your life what you attract and believe in. This is a characteristic one must include in their daily meditation and journaling, and I shall include this later in the book. Self-esteem may be boosted by encouraging the belief that you can do anything.

This reinforcement boosts your self-esteem, which is necessary for you to advance in your career. To be successful, you must embrace this self-esteem and trust in yourself, and you must adopt it by expecting the proper things to come your way. Simply concentrate on your work and strive to fulfill deadlines as efficiently as possible while maintaining confidence in your abilities and believe me when I say that you will noticeably improve.

What are the ways you feel you can improve in your career? Are you struggling with meeting deadlines, or do you feel like certain tasks are your weakness because you lack skills?

_____

_____

_____

_____

_____

TIP: If you know you need to develop skills to be successful, do not be afraid to reach out to your departmental manager or your HR department. Start online courses or government-funded courses. Remember that the skills you gather will remain yours wherever you will go, and this will never be taken away from you. If you hold a managerial position and although you do have the skills you need to complete a particular task that you struggle with, feel free to delegate it if possible. There is nothing wrong with asking for help or recognizing that you need to brush up on your skills.

People are happy because of the joyful times they have had in their life. Similarly, expecting good things in the future may have a pleasant and enjoyable influence on us. If you try to discover something nice and positive in every circumstance, you will gradually begin to feel genuine happiness as you eliminate unpleasant ideas from your head. You'll feel revitalized, energized, and enthusiastic about solving your issues in a more effective manner.

Motivation is a key component in achieving exceptional results in life, and we may attain it by cultivating a positive attitude in life. Failures are a part of life, therefore don't be discouraged by them.

Instead, anticipate something positive to happen every day of your life by thinking that you can succeed with one more try. This thought pattern provides you with the inspiration and encouragement you need to finish a task successfully. According to current studies, having optimistic aspirations in life improves both your mental and physical health. Aggression, sadness, and poor health are the result of negative ideas and hopelessness.

On the other side, the more positive you believe, the better your immune system will be since negative hormones will be reduced in your body. A good attitude and aspirations can help to prevent a variety of psychosomatic and organic illnesses.

9) Take care of your self-esteem!

Start addressing any areas that are bothering you once you've begun checking in with yourself. Internal issues can often lead to low self-esteem; therefore, it's important to spend time taking care of yourself. Treating oneself like you would a beloved friend in a pleasant but honest manner is the greatest approach to boost your self-esteem. This is an excellent method to assess how you care for yourself, particularly if you are a freelancer or a self-employed.

Thinking of yourself as your best manager or best friend might help you reframe your relationship with yourself and enable you to be nicer and fairer to yourself. Furthermore, even at work, allow yourself to be vulnerable. Noticing your problem areas or your flaws is a crucial first step in getting help or overcoming your problems entirely. Rather than comparing yourself to others, try to focus on your own objectives and accomplishments. That type of stress is unnecessary! Exercise is a great way to enhance motivation, practice discipline, and develop confidence.

Breaking a sweat also causes the release of feel-good chemicals known as endorphins. Always strive to be the finest possible version of yourself. You make mistakes in order to learn and grow, therefore don't be too hard on yourself.

Concentrate your attention on deciding which areas of your life are under your control and what you can do about them. Spending time doing activities you enjoy makes you more likely to think positively. Make an effort to make time for yourself every day. Make time for whatever brings you joy, whether it's reading, cooking, or simply sitting on the couch.

What makes you happy? What is the ONE activity you will now be setting time aside to take care of your self-esteem and self-care?

_____

_____

_____

_____

_____

(10) Stop hunting down happiness!

Take pride in your job, your life, and your achievements. You can discover satisfaction by just thinking about past events, some of which were accomplishments and others that were simply enjoyable. Try reflecting on your experience on a frequent basis if you're a freelancer or entrepreneur. It's easy to overthink about the future and forget how well you've done in the past. You'll not only be able to relive the feelings that milestones produced, but you'll also be able to improve yourself and your business by focusing on your prior experiences.

I saved the best for last; many individuals associate happiness with achieving specific objectives or desires. Happiness becomes a reward rather than an emotion that deserves to be felt daily because of this practice. Allow yourself to enjoy happiness whenever it comes your way, rather than pursuing objectives that may give you temporary happiness. Make happiness a state of mind, and the following chapter will give you a good start on the habits you can start adopting to enhance your happiness.

CHAPTER 9: CULTIVATING HAPPINESS

Our habits reflect our mood and state of mind, from waking up in the morning to the work we do and the food we eat. The way we react to situations and circumstances has a cascading effect, which leads to a change or a result. And we're making a lot of decisions every day, creating or maintaining habits, and attempting to have a good mindset in the process. Our behaviors cause changes in our lives, some positive and others negative. We live in a world where many bad, frightening, controversial, and frequently bizarre events occur. What we hear on the news, on social media, and on the radio is constantly bombarding us, and it's tough not to internalize it all.

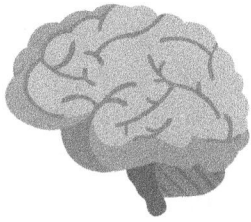

Our brains process a tremendous amount of stuff at the speed of light, attempting to sort out the positive, the negative, and the neutral. Our habits mould us and influence how we view the events in our lives. It's critical to develop cheerful habits that allow you to maintain mental peace.

Mental health or self-check-ins should be done every day, especially if you suffer from depression or anxiety. You are free to do whatever you want during these check-ins.

💡 TIP: Check in with yourself every day. The swiftest way to do this is via a daily journal, where you evaluate your morning and plan. You can do a follow-up check-in in the evening to evaluate your day and tick the goals you managed to accomplish from the morning. This will give you such a clear perspective in the morning and such a relief in the evening if you have managed to tick all your boxes. If not, you know what you need to start with the next morning, and you can also use this time to find what goes in the way of accomplishing your goals.

Happy habits have the capacity to provide you joy that lasts a lifetime. Adopting cheerful habits will improve your outlook and how you respond to life's events and transitions. Here are some ideas for healthy habits you can start incorporating to increase your happiness:

💡 The sun makes us cheerful. When UV rays strike the skin, the body produces vitamin D. Vitamin D insufficiency has been linked to depression and other mental illnesses. When sunshine reaches your eyes, it sends a signal to your brain to reduce the secretion of melatonin, a hormone that aids sleep, while increasing the secretion of serotonin, a hormone linked to happiness and alertness. Even in the winter, regardless of how cold it is, I will go outside and spend time walking in nature. I've developed a habit of going for nature walks, listening to my footsteps, inhaling fresh air, and staring at nature. I will concentrate on sounds outside if I am having a stressful or difficult day. I pay attention to all my senses. My thoughts are soothed by calmness.

💡 To do something creative, you don't have to be creative. If your thoughts are driving you crazy, try coloring in adult coloring books. Sudoku puzzles and word searches are two activities I enjoy doing to distract myself from the stress of daily living. The mind is quieted by undertaking puzzle-like activities if this is something you think you will enjoy doing.

You'll immediately set the tone for a stress-free day if you spend only fifteen minutes a day cleaning and tidying your living room, kitchen, or bedroom. I was able to make more time for building those positive habits that promote my mental health after I started investing fifteen minutes each evening in cleaning. Cleaning can be therapeutic or meditative. Keeping your living space in order will allow you to devote more time to work or other duties. If, like me you feel that cleaning the entire house at once is too much of a task, this will work magic.

Even ten minutes of quiet or solitude can have a positive impact on your mental and emotional health. Simply sit somewhere comfy with your eyes closed for ten minutes and conduct breathing exercises. If you're especially flustered or stressed, you might also try a quick self-hypnosis session. With these ten minutes of stillness, you can create your own schedule. When I've had this period of silence, I'm able to produce my greatest work. It's a tiny thing you can do that will help you in the long run, and it's a way to give balance to your day. I tend to incorporate this during my morning routine, and I use it to meditate at the same time.

While meditation has a spiritual and odd reputation among people who do not practice it, it provides benefits for almost everyone who gives it a fair chance. Meditation does not strike me as spiritual. It's therapeutic, in my opinion. Every day, I sit quietly for five to ten minutes and focus on myself. I close my eyes occasionally and don't at other times. But I concentrate on my breathing, assess how I'm feeling, and imagine how my day will unfold. Give it a shot. You will not be displeased.

◎ CHALLENGE 15

Take a deep breath and sit up straight. Pull your shoulders back. Repeat the process a few more times. The way you stand and breathe has a big impact on how you feel about life. Taking shallow, weak breaths can deplete your vital energy. You'll be happy throughout the day if you sit up straight with your shoulders back and take deep breaths as often as possible.

Keep a daily journal or log of what you accomplished that day and what you need to accomplish the next day. If you're someone who is rough on yourself or puts a lot of responsibility on yourself, this type of writing will change your outlook on how you're doing in life. It's a technique for unloading your workload on paper and seeing it for what it is: straightforward and simple. Keeping a log will lighten the weights off your shoulders and lessen the stress and tension on your thoughts if you have a truckload of things to do or things you forget to do. It will rebuild your brain and mind while leaving your emotions intact, allowing you to perform at your best. At the same time, it will assist you in staying on track.

You'll be less inattentive and more aware of what you need to accomplish to get to the finish line of work or other tasks. I tend to keep a section for checklists in my journal and keep it next to my bed because I tend to get a lot of thoughts of things I must do and ideas late at night. This way, you can just dump your ideas on a piece of paper, allowing you to get a restful sleep.

I've been doing fifteen minutes of stretching every day for three years and counting, and it's still going strong. There's no need to do yoga or twist yourself like a buddha. I'm referring to simple stretching that anyone can do. Stretching daily will benefit your health, improve your sleep, and relieve muscle tightness, strain, and tension. Because all my stress is concentrated in my shoulders and back, I'll spend fifteen minutes stretching, either light or deep, to relax and unwind. When your body is taken care of, your mind will be lighter. Stretching has a variety of health perks, including reducing fatigue, sleeplessness, and stress. Focusing on how you feel physically is a fantastic place to start if you want to transform your outlook and your life.

Food is happiness, and what you eat has an impact on how you feel. While it's fine to treat yourself to a milkshake or brownies every now and then, studies now suggest that sugar, gluten, and dairy are linked to sadness and anxiety. These can cause exhaustion or a breakdown, as they strain your system. I set a goal for myself to achieve a habit of making tiny, bowl-sized salads that take five minutes to prepare and don't require any culinary abilities. I choose three veggies and one fruit, all of which include spinach or other greens. I've seen a major shift in my general mood since I started making salads every day. Clean eating is an excellent habit to incorporate into your routine because it improves happiness.

I've resolved to volunteer as often as my schedule permits. Trust me when I confess my schedule is always crammed. However, being away from the boring tasks I perform while I volunteer me feel calmer and happier. Volunteering and giving to others have been tremendously motivating, rewarding, and enlightening for me, even though I enjoy my job. You'll notice that you're more relaxed, less rushed, and have more opportunities to appreciate others and life. This adds to the act of kindness I discussed earlier. Abandoned animals and underprivileged children or women are some of the things I value the most, so I volunteer with organizations that hold the same values as me.

Participate in a community enrichment class, such as cooking, sewing, yoga, a reading club, or arts and crafts. Many cities even provide enjoyable initiatives for persons in their field of work. Even if it's only once a month, do something out of your comfort zone. I know people who work forty hours a week and still find time to participate in an enrichment program. Someone I know uses their lunch break to keep fit and exercise so that they can return to work refreshed. Doing things like that will add variety to your day and make you eager to return to work.

On your way to work, you were cut off. You've been issued a citation. The strange part about not being happy when these things happen is that you have no control over it. You've decided to allow outside factors to determine how you feel about life. The world transforms when you realize you have influence over these things by simply shifting your attitude. Consider the situation where you were cut off on your way to work. You overlook their conduct and are not negatively affected by it if you make an excuse for them, such as they are rushing to get their pregnant wife to the hospital. Hopefully, they arrive at the hospital in time and give birth to a beautiful child. Perspective is everything!

Lists of your life are fantastic. They're like an amusement park for people who want to organize their lives. Consider the things you'd like to see and do before you pass away. It can be life-changing and inspiring, especially if you create plans to start crossing items off your life list.

Hobbies are enjoyable methods to find happiness. Whether you enjoy cooking, playing games, painting, or anything else, learning a new hobby is a rewarding experience. Focus on the pleasure of simply trying something new when beginning a new pastime. There's something amazing about being a novice because there's something to learn from every experience.

Learning to appreciate what you have is a prize in and of itself. People who express gratitude and take the time to be grateful are happier and have more optimistic perspectives on life.

TIP: Begin with a straightforward task. Think of what happened during the day that you are thankful for every night before you go to bed. Write it down. It won't be long before that habit transforms your entire outlook.

One of the most powerful provocateurs of happiness is fear. Fear makes us worry, which causes tension and a negative mindset. Begin to welcome fear into your life to overcome it. Obviously, you don't want to dive right in, but start small and face your worries. With each fear conquered, you'll get stronger, more confident, and happier.

I have traveled and know that this isn't a universal practice, but I believe it should be. Smiling is simple to perform, feels good, communicates happiness to your brain, and can be the only cheerful thing the recipient of your smile sees that day. With only a flash of your pearly whites, you can brighten the lives of those around you.

Some people believe that swallowing and suppressing their bad thoughts and feelings will make them happier. Unfortunately, it always seems to resurface, showing itself as tension, bodily pain, or other forms of discomfort. The reality is that with negativity, it is vital to recognize and accept that awful things do happen from time to time. You will be stressed at times. Things happen to you that you have no control over at times. Understanding and embracing this will relieve the stress you are experiencing because of your repression. This allows you to return to the things that bring you joy.

Setting a high standard and then exceeding it is one of the most rewarding things you can do in life. By setting ambitions for yourself that are realistic yet demand effort, you will continue to work hard and develop, frequently leading to a feeling of success rather than satisfaction with the progress you've achieved simply by having the objective. Set difficult goals for yourself, and then plan to achieve them. Every accomplishment serves as a steppingstone toward your best, happiest self.

You must nourish your mind on a regular basis to maintain a happy mindset. Calm is achieved through lifestyle activities such as attentive meditation, planting one's feet on the ground and focusing on one's breathing, or contemplative strolling. Getting adequate sunlight nourishes the brain, increases serotonin production, and listening to nature sounds counteracts negative thoughts.

When starting a new habit, think about how it will affect your health or attitude in life in the long run. If you're trying to break a habit that's sabotaging your happiness, replace it with a tiny habit. Instead of putting pressure on yourself, the goal is to explore and improve. You shouldn't be afraid of change; it should inspire you and lead you along a more rewarding and useful path.

Write down at least five key concepts you learned from reading this chapter.

_____

_____

_____

_____

_____

_____

_____

_____

_____

CHAPTER 10:
HAPPINESS EXERCISES

After the knowledge you have gathered about happiness so far, you are very likely to be capable of conducting the following exercises easily. This workbook has led you to reformulate your thinking, and here are some exercises you can do to increase your happiness. These exercises vary from journaling, breathing techniques to an actual set schedule you can follow if your routine permits it.

Daily Exercises

Spot something beautiful in your environment. Take time to look around you and find beauty in five things and list them below. ✍

Focus your attention on your senses and whatever surrounds you. This can be anything from smells you enjoy, sights, sensations, and even tastes. Do you this as often as you please. This will help you to train your senses to experience happiness in the things you overlook every day.

🕐 *Take ten minutes to identify one important life event. Give it a title below.* ✍

Jot down the positive effects this event has left on you, and make sure you talk about this in detail. This will take you five minutes from the entire exercise. ✍

_____

_____

_____

_____

_____

_____

_____

_____

_____

🕐 *Now that you have listed all the positive effects this event has left on you, take a few minutes to contemplate on your life if it had to be without this event. This exercise is designed to enhance the attitude of contentment and appreciation about the world around us.*

List five acts of kindness you intend to do in one day. ✒

The goal of this exercise is to spread the act of kindness to those you come across. Any gesture counts from giving small gifts to holding a door open.

IIf you need to apologize to someone, make sure you apologize because you acknowledge the mistake and seek responsibility for it. You must express remorse and offer redress for this to be truthful. Make sure you commit to not repeating the same mistake again and have empathy for the other individual.

After you have apologized, focus on the impact it has on both sides. The idea behind this is to cultivate happiness and pride.

IThink of something that did not go so well for you; maybe you burnt your veggies today whilst making lunch, or you failed to land an interview you have meant to pass successfully. Do not try to suppress the feelings this unpleasant situation caused you. List three positive things you could have gained in this activity was successful.

After accepting you have failed at this task, identify the skills you think you could develop to do better next time.

_____

_____

_____

_____

You can do this for every big goal you have in life that somehow seems to never come true because something is always getting in the way. This can help you become more optimistic and instill hope in you.

Breathing Exercises

A few deep breaths can solve a lot of problems. Really. Controlled breathing exercises are a simple, quick, and effective approach to relieve stress and tension, enhance confidence, relieve muscle tension and pain, improve attention, lower blood pressure, and produce an overall sense of calm. And various breathing exercises can produce various levels of well-being. So, take a moment and slow down. Do a mindful breathing exercise.

The enhanced mood breathing exercise
1. Close your eyes and place one hand in the center of your chest and the other over your belly button while sitting up straight on a chair or on the floor.
2. Take an eight-count deep breath in through your nose, feeling your tummy expand as you do so.
3. Count to eight while holding your breath.
4. Slowly exhale through your nose for a count of ten.
5. Repeat three times more.

A breathing exercise to keep your temper under control.
Resist the urge to become enraged. Take a deep, thorough inhale from your lower belly and come to a complete stop. Out through the mouth, inhale through the nose.
1. Do it again.
2. Say or repeat a calming word or phrase, such as "relax" or "it'll be OK."
3. Remind yourself that you have control over your reactions and that the trigger that sets off your rage isn't worth sacrificing your peace of mind for.

A breathing exercise to keep your temper under control.
1. Cross your legs at the ankles or cross one leg over the other and sit on the floor. Close your eyes. Sit up straight. Place your hands on your knees.
2. Take several slow, deep breaths in and out.
3. Exhale gently through your nostrils on the following deep breath, keeping your lips closed, teeth slightly apart, and generating a humming sound as you do so.
4. Inhale deeply through your nose without humming, then exhale slowly while humming.
5. Repeat the above steps ten times.

Breathing Exercise to promote focus
1. Raise your right hand and place your thumb against your right nostril while keeping your mouth closed for the duration of the exercise. Your index and middle fingers can rest on the space between your brows. With your right thumb, cover your right nostril. Slowly exhale through the left nostril.

2. Inhale slowly through your left nostril while still holding your right thumb over your right nostril.

3. Raise your right thumb away from your right nose and cover your left nostril with your right hand's pinkie finger. Exhale slowly through your right nostril. Then take a deep breath via your right nostril.

4. Repeat the technique nine times after you've completed one full round of exhaling, then in from one nostril and then the other.

The exercise that will help you wake up

1. Breathe slowly and deeply through your nose.

2. Exhale through your nose in one rapid, strong movement, focusing on releasing the breath from your lower belly. At all times during the activity, keep your mouth shut.

3. Because the workout is mostly focused on the stomach muscles, it may appear awkward at first.

4. For a total of 10 breaths, repeat this process of inhaling and exhaling through your nose, pausing for one to two seconds after each exhale.

The energizing breathing technique

1. Keep your back straight either on the floor with your legs folded under you or at the edge of a chair.

2. Raise your arms to your sides, arms bent, and hands in loose fists beside your shoulders. Inhale deeply, then exhale slowly.

3. Raise your arms straight up to your shoulders and open your palms wide as you inhale deeply through your nose. Breathe out quickly and forcefully through your nostrils as your arms return to their original posture by your sides, hands closing.

3. Raise your arms straight up to your shoulders and open your palms wide as you inhale deeply through your nose. Breathe out quickly and forcefully through your nostrils as your arms return to their original posture by your sides, hands closing.

4. Continue to breathe slowly and steadily through your nose for around Fifteen breaths. Then unwind. Rep the entire pattern three times more, but don't go any further. Reduce if you feel light-headed. If you are pregnant, avoid this exercise altogether.

The equal breathing techniques especially intended for beginners

1. Begin with adjusting your breathing to get the life balance you desire. Simply take four seconds to inhale and four seconds to exhale. This is all done through the nose and not through the mouth.

2. When you feel comfortable with this, aim for six to eight seconds per breath.

This method is handy when you need to unwind before going to bed or immediately before a stressful event. It assists you in being focused on the subject at hand without allowing your thoughts to wander.

The yoga breathing technique

1. Close your eyes and lie down on a bed or other comfortable surface, arms at your sides and legs relaxed naturally.
2. Breathe through your nose a few times, then tighten your neck so you can hear your breath coming in and out. It's almost like when someone relaxes before going to sleep and starts snoring.
3. Start with breathing in for a count of four and out for a count of four for a few breaths, then gradually increase the length of the breaths in and out to six counts.
4. Increase to Eight counts, then Ten counts, depending on your comfort level, and repeat before going back down to an 8-count breath cycle, then a six-count breath cycle, and finally a four-count breath cycle.

The 4-7-8 breathing technique

This well-known breathing technique is performed while sitting up in bed or on the floor with crossed legs and back straight.

1. Gently press your tongue against the ridge behind your teeth for the duration of the workout.
2. Begin by exhaling through your lips to empty your lungs.
3. Close your mouth and inhale for four counts through your nose, then hold for seven counts. Make a whooshing sound by exhaling for a count of 8 through your mouth while keeping your tongue in place.
4. Rep this cycle 4-6 times more.

The chest breathing technique

Instead of breathing deeply through the belly and diaphragm as is normally recommended for healthy breathing, you can breathe via the top of the chest, which requires the body to rely on muscles that aren't used as frequently when breathing. When you breathe via your chest, you engage several muscles that you don't normally use, such as those in your neck. As a result, they receive a good workout.

However, get into the practice of breathing from your diaphragm rather than your chest, as too much chest breathing can exacerbate neck and shoulder tension, which is prevalent among office workers. A weak diaphragm will readily exhaust during activity, resulting in a lack of blood flow to your muscles during your next gym session or workout.

The double breathing technique

1. If counting in and out isn't your thing, try exhaling twice as long as you inhale. Sit or lie down according to your preference.
2. Count or estimate how long it takes you to inhale, then exhale for twice that amount of time.

The meditative-type breathing

With meditative breathing, you can eliminate the counting. All you must do is sit comfortably with your legs crossed and your back straight, your hands on your knees lightly.

1. For the next ten minutes, your main emphasis should be on noticing your breath. Allow your thoughts to pass and refocus your attention on how your lungs fill and empty with each inhale and exhale.
2. If you want, you can select a guided meditation app, a video, or another source to help you relax before bed.
3. The idea is to keep an eye on your breathing and pay attention to it. Do not try to change it, and don't try to prevent it from changing; things can change simply by being observed. Allow your body to do the breathing as you relax and enjoy it.

The progressive breathing technique

1. Close your eyes and concentrate on tensing and relaxing each muscle group for two to three seconds each to relieve any tension from head to toe.
2. Begin with the feet and toes, then work your way up to the knees, thighs, back, chest, arms, hands, neck, jaw, and eyes while breathing deeply and slowly.
3. It is recommended to breathe in via the nose, holding for a count of five as the muscles tense, and then breathing out through the mouth on release.
4. Exhale each time you release muscle tension and allow the muscle to loosen and soften before moving on to the next muscle. As you practice, you can be broader or more particular. You can also use visualization, as indicated below; envision colors or feelings as you exhale, and the muscles soften.

The visualized breathing technique

1. As you breathe, imagine yourself in a safe and comfortable atmosphere, and correlate your nice breathing with a soothing environment.
1. Then imagine yourself in various life scenarios or hard environments while continuing to breathe in a comfortable manner. Not only will this assist you in desensitizing tension or anxiety about certain occurrences, but it will also provide you with a useful tool to use when that situation arises.

3. Simply begin to breathe in the manner you have practiced, and your intensity levels will be balanced and optimal.

Wim Hof's method

Wim Hof is known as The Iceman because of his incredible and insane feats with ice water, climbing mountains in shorts, and generally being unfazed by the cold. Through the pillars of cold treatment, breathwork, and commitment training, he has established his own technique for enhancing the lives of others. This technique is said to help with stress, resilience and aids in the release of energy.

1. Sit or lie down to get comfortable.
2. Deeply inhale through your nose or mouth. Inhale completely through the abdominal button. Allow yourself to let go naturally.
3. In brief, strong bursts, repeat 30–40 times.
4. Hold. Inhale one last time after the last expiration and hold your breath for as long as you can.
5. Take a deep breath to recover and hold it for 15 seconds to fill your lungs.
6. Steps one to four should be repeated three to four times more.

The box breathing method

Mark Divine is a former Seal commander who founded several organizations dedicated to mind and body training for peak performance. The box breathing method is one of his strategies.

1. Inhale deeply for 4 seconds until your lungs are totally filled.
2. Four seconds of holding your breath
3. Exhale until your lungs are completely empty.
4. Hold the position for 4 seconds.
5. Repeat three times more. This training can be done for 10 to 20 minutes daily.

The three-part breathing technique

Among other things, diaphragmatic breathing has been demonstrated to ease emotional stress. It's your body's natural breathing pattern, but it's typically suppressed by stressed-out chest breathing. The three-part breath takes use of the diaphragmatic breathing pattern by utilizing the entire capacity of your lungs.

1. Lying down, sitting, or standing are all options. For newbies to breath-work, lying down is the most pleasant and simple way. Lie down comfortably on your back with both hands on your tummy, the tips of your middle fingers touching.
2. Lift and squeeze your belly button into your hands while inhaling. Carry on like this until your fingertips are no longer touching.

3. Exhale, allowing your tummy to drop and your fingers to reconnect. Repeat this process two more times.

4. Move your hands to cup your ribcage on the outside. Your fingers will no longer touch. Inhale as you did before, pressing your belly button up.

5. Take another breath and draw it to your center torso, squeezing your rib cage into your hands. Feel your ribs return to neutral and your tummy collapse as you exhale. Rep this process one or two more times.

6. Cross your arms across your chest. Inhale, pressing your belly button up, and then extend through your ribcage, like you did just a few moments before.

7. Take the third sip of air and drag it toward your chest, causing it to rise beneath your palms.

8. Exhale, allowing your chest to drop, your ribs to return to neutral, and your belly to deflate.

9. Continue to breathe normally as in the steps above but move your hands to any portion of your torso in any combination. If you want, take at least another ten breaths this way.

Breathing techniques may improve your life in a variety of ways and learning to use your breath in situations where you need to lower stress or boost attention can help you in almost every situation. Breathing deliberately affects your nervous system and lessens tension. Breathing boosts the production of leptins, which reduce appetite and improve exercise stamina, as well as the diaphragm muscles and lung capacity. Breathing exercises might cause you to pass out or become disoriented, so make sure you practice in a safe place. Never do breathwork in the bath or anywhere else where fainting is a risk.

Physical Exercise

That post-workout feeling. The prospect of that feeling can be enough to bring you to the gym. You could call that feeling an endorphin surge, which isn't entirely inaccurate, but exercise makes you happier in a variety of ways. Exercise lowers stress levels, reducing feelings of loneliness and isolation, and aiding in the relief of anxiety and depression, among other things.

The act of moving leads you to connect with others. That's just the way the brain works. When you raise your heart rate, use your body, and use your muscles, your brain chemistry transforms in a way that makes it easier to connect with others, bond with them, and trust them. It improves social joys.

Because of the way exercise improves our brain chemistry and viewpoint, you begin to feel a true feeling of connection with the individuals you're moving with, whether it's a walking group or a group class. It's why people refer to their fitness family as the people with whom they exercise. It helps us develop relationships that can be true friendships and sources of support since it gives us a sense of belonging. When you connect with others who share your values, such as appreciating your health and wellness and having interests in whatever form of workout you do, your friendship is naturally strengthened because you share these beliefs.

Exercise increases endorphins, dopamine, adrenaline, and endocannabinoids, which are all brain chemicals linked to feelings of happiness, confidence, capability, reduced anxiety and stress and even reduced physical pain. Exercise has also been demonstrated to aid in the treatment of depression in some people, which scientists believe is related to an increase in nerve cell growth in the brain that occurs when you exercise. Myokine, which your body produces when your muscles contract, is another hormone that has been shown to help relieve stress and enhance happiness. These myokines begin to alter the function and structure of your brain, making you more resistant to stress and potentially aiding recovery from depression and anxiety disorders. Confidence is essential for feeling happier and more empowered in life.

Exercise might help you feel more confident since you're doing something strenuous with other people. This gives you a sense of shared accomplishment and collaboration. Exercising outside has a profound instant influence on mood, especially for despair and anxiety. Because it generates a state of open awareness in your brain that is quite a like meditation, for people whose minds aren't their best pals and who struggle with negative thinking and worry, something as simple as going for a walk or riding a bike outside can have an immediate, profound effect that can provide tremendous relief because it invites the mind to shift spontaneously and without effort.

Physically active individuals feel a sense of success in accomplishing personal fitness objectives in addition to greater energy. They may also be pleased with their enhanced physical appearance because of their gym time. Getting outside on a lovely day, or even working out indoors with a group of strangers, stimulates the mind and shakes up what might be a tedious and fully enclosed daily routine for some people. Exercise has been demonstrated to help insomniacs' sleep patterns. In the area of the brain responsible for learning and memory, exercise is also important for the formation of new brain cells.

Antibodies are raised because of both exercise and happiness. People who are joyful are more resistant to diseases ranging from the common cold to heart disease, whereas people who are stressed and anxious are more prone to illnesses such as diabetes and stroke. Exercise-induced pleasure enhances the immune system independently of the physiological effects of the exercise because persons who exercise report higher levels of happiness.

One of these side effects is a decrease in cortisol levels in the body; a hormone released when the body is stressed. It boosts the immune system in small doses, but too much diminishes your ability to fight illness. The fact that exercise lowers cortisol levels in the body may also explain why it makes you feel less anxious.

Happiness and exercise are strikingly similar in two ways: both are linked to a boost in the immune response and the production of endorphins. Exercise is another stress-reduction and mood-improvement method that not only appears to make individuals happier but also has good long-term benefits that are more conducive to long-term happiness. Whether it's a walk outdoors, a group hike, or a bike ride, make physical activity a daily habit. My best solution for adapting this habit is enrolling in a few classes at first until I got to enjoy exercising again. Once that became something I looked forward to, I started switching my training regime between spinning classes, group classes, yoga sessions, and individual sessions at the gym. Alongside a healthy diet, physical activity can truly maximize your happiness levels.

Adult Coloring

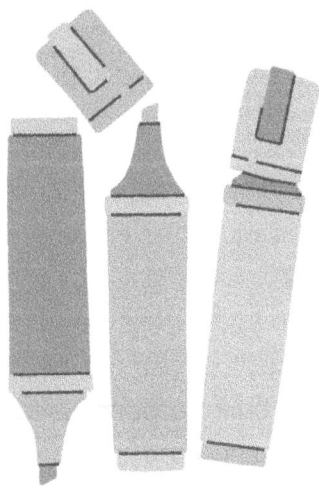

Do you think coloring for hours is only something kids do? Reconsider! Adult coloring books have been popular across the world, with some even making bestseller lists. With the numerous health advantages of adult coloring, it's time to break out the crayons, colored pencils, and markers!

There are significant distinctions between coloring books for children and coloring books for adults, despite their many similarities. Adult coloring books are typically designed with a specific goal in mind. Colouring books for kids are typically meant to educate kids on how to color within the lines while still being creative. Adult coloring books, on the other hand, are typically about health and wellbeing.

Adult coloring books, for example, frequently include patterns that are intended to relieve tension and anxiety. In certain cases, they may feature elaborate patterns and ornamental embellishments that are intended to help develop fine motor skills. Adult coloring books may also be used to acquire new abilities and to aid those with concentration problems by lengthening their attention span.

Here are some benefits of adult coloring in relation to happiness:

- ☑ The amygdala, your brain's fear center, may be calmed by coloring. By decreasing the ideas of a restless mind, it creates the same sensation as meditation. After a hard day at work, this promotes awareness and silence, allowing your mind to relax.

- ☑ Colouring is more than just a pleasurable way to unwind. It necessitates communication between the two hemispheres of the brain. Choosing colors produces a creative cognitive process, but logic helps us stay inside the lines.

- ☑ Because exposure to the emitted light decreases your levels of the sleep hormone melatonin, we know we get a better night's sleep when we avoid engaging with gadgets at night. Colouring is a soothing, electronic-free night routine that won't interfere with your melatonin levels.

- ☑ Adult coloring can help relieve tension. Colouring is relaxing; soothing nature may go a long way toward assisting people in coping with anxiety and bad emotions. They're for, and color therapy may be a powerful tool for reducing and soothing anxiety. This is a simple exercise that takes total concentration, and it can help individuals cope with anxiety in a constructive way.

- ☑ There aren't many hobbies that engage the full brain, but coloring is one of them. Colouring isn't a right or left-brain activity. This is a job that necessitates the cooperation of both hemispheres of the brain. As a result, coloring is a complete brain workout.

- ☑ You must color slowly and deliberately to properly complete your adult coloring book. This is a crucial practice that will help you discover more about yourself as a person.

- ☑ Adult coloring books are a great way to keep your mind active. As a result, you may be less likely to acquire some types of dementia in the future. You may be able to avoid the onset of certain chronic neurological disorders if you train your mind on a regular basis.

☑ Adult coloring books will allow you to understand more about yourself, even if you don't consider yourself to be very artistic. Adult coloring books challenge you to concentrate all your energy and attention on the present moment. Then you must embrace your work without hesitation or judgment. Adult coloring books are a fantastic place to start if you want to discover more about yourself. As you work your way through adult coloring books, you may come across designs that are increasingly difficult. You must concentrate on what you're doing, shut off the outside world, and learn new abilities. Furthermore, no matter how chaotic the world may seem, adult coloring books may encourage you to slow down.

☑ Adult coloring books are said to educate you to pay attention to details, which is one of the primary therapeutic advantages. Intricate patterns abound in many adult coloring books. If you want to finish the design properly, you must concentrate on minor lines. Adult coloring books are a fantastic place to start if you want to learn to pay more attention to details.

☑ When you color in adult coloring books, you may sometimes unleash your inner child. You could recall a few nice childhood memories while you do so. One of the characteristics of kids is that they enjoy the simple things in life. As an adult, you can have the same experience. If you genuinely appreciate adult coloring books, you could find that you are happier today than you were previously.

☑ When you color in adult coloring books, you may sometimes unleash your inner child. You could recall a few nice childhood memories while you do so. One of the characteristics of kids is that they enjoy the simple things in life. As an adult, you can have the same experience. If you genuinely appreciate adult coloring books, you could find that you are happier today than you were previously.

One of the most significant advantages of adult coloring books is this. You can get the most out of your adult coloring experience if you can recall a few childhood experiences. This also ties in how cherishing the little things in life and allowing ourselves to celebrate them as kids do. I have also mentioned how memories can also bring back happiness, although not living them in real-time, and this can help with all this.

You don't need to be a professional artist to color! If you're for an entertaining way to unwind after a long day at work, coloring is a great way to start. Choose whatever you like and color it in any way you want!

Meditation

Developing an underlying sense of pleasure and fulfillment does not always translate into a wide-eyed, exploding type of bliss. Rather, it is a reunion with our mind's joyful state that leads to this true sensation of fulfillment and reconnection with something intrinsic inside us. We create the conditions for experiencing a pleasant state of mind by practicing meditation for pleasure and happiness.

It has long been assumed that each of us has a happiness set point or a fixed average level of happiness that we are born with, but owing to neuroplasticity, the setpoint may be changed. You can retrain your brain to reset its happy set point by meditating. According to research, this is accomplished by thickening the key parts of the brain responsible for assisting you in dealing with stressful events, as well as decreasing the amygdala, the portion of the brain that is engaged when you are stressed.

Living in fear of happiness has been linked to anxiety and despair, according to studies. You may reduce your chances of anxiety and depression by taking the time to cultivate your mind and being more receptive to the concept of happiness. Living a happy life and letting go of your connection to external events might help you feel less stressed and enjoy a better night's sleep.

Try the following meditation routines while putting on meditation background music :

☑ Make yourself comfortable. Feel free to lie down or be seated. Adjust your posture in any way that allows you to feel at ease in your body. You may close your eyes and soften the muscles in your face. Release your jaw and settle into a comfortable position. Release your tension. If you notice a tight posture in your hips or in your arms, allow it to soften and relax your body.

Check-in with yourself, your emotions, and how you are feeling. Prepare your mind for acceptance, accepting whatever comes your way because by now, you have established that even in the negative occurrences, you can still find the positive little things. Remember that your intention for this meditation is to feel motivated and joyful. Start focusing on your breathing and acknowledge it. Inhale, and your body will expand and open. Once you exhale, let go. Keep your focus shifted on your breathing.

Relaxation takes over your body; allow it. Soften the tight grips you have anywhere that is tensed. Your body is left doing what it is meant to do naturally, relax and breathe. You will notice that the area in your chest expands when inhaling. While you exhale, your body releases and sinks down. Here you should be letting go of whatever is weighing you down. Your breath is a tool to surrender and relax; embrace this. Each breath is a loving experience for yourself.

Maintain calmness throughout this exercise. Imagine a loved one or a friend that often brings a smile to your face when you simply think of them. This is someone that is easy to love, and the love you have for them is easy and natural. They should be people that bring joy to you. Bring the energy they bring and the image of their face to your mind. While you inhale, allow the love you feel for them to expand with your breathing.

Feel joy and happiness from this person whilst recalling a particular experience you had with them. If your mind goes to wonder, allow the happiness and joy this person brings to you to help you shift your focus back to this meditation session. Imagine experiencing happiness with this person. Synchronise your positive energies together. Your happiness continues as is and grows. Wish you could live with gratitude and kindness forever.

Acknowledge that you can appreciate the joy in your life. Now, shift your focus on yourself. You have created a positive vibe with the help of the positive people in your life you consider a blessing. Think of the times you as an individual has experienced joy and happiness. Experience the sensation of joy starting from your heart and going throughout your body.

Send positive affirmations to yourself and allow yourself to appreciate the happiness in your life. May this positive continue to prosper and grow. May you appreciate every little thing in your life. May you be able to conquer every negative outcome in your life and let happiness prosper. If your mind trails off, allow yourself to come back to the happiness you have created in your heart. Allow this gratitude and happiness in your body to expand, flowing from your heart. Let this positivity expand to the people around you, your friends, your family, and the rest of the world.

The joy you cultivated is now radiating outwards towards those around you, far or near. Acknowledge how you started at the beginning of this meditation session and where you made it to now. Understand that you can create this environment for yourself.

You can cultivate happiness anything you want. Start smiling; notice how your mouth and eyes lift to create a positive smile on your face. This is the joyful smile you created. Start to move your fingers and your body slowly, whilst your smile increases. Slowly, open your eyes and let your joy and happiness grow after this meditation session, with a simple smile.

☑ Switch off from all the noise and sit comfortably to start this next meditation session. Sit comfortably with your feet touching the floor. Relax your face. Straighten your back and relax your body. Rest your hands with your palms facing upwards on your knees. Close your eyes if you wish or if that does not feel comfortable, lower your gaze to your hands on your knees. Inhale and exhale, emptying your lungs whilst your shoulders relax. Inhale and breath out again. Wish yourself health, happiness, and peace. Repeat this in your mind if your mind is wandering off to someplace else; bring these wishes back to your mind and repeat them until your focus is shifted to meditation again. Allow yourself to feel the way you are manifesting as you repeat those wishes to yourself. Shift your focus to a loved one, a close family member, or a close friend. Think of them.

Send loving kindness to them. Wish them the same things you wished yourself earlier; may they be happy, healthy, and peaceful. Allow these words to reach them and send positivity to them across the distance. Let these positive vibrations reach out to your community. As these positive affirmations reach out to the world, you should feel a more loving atmosphere. Start to bring your attention back to reality. Slowly open your eyes and bring your gaze straight ahead. Allow the compassion and loving atmosphere you created for the rest of the day.

☑ This meditation exercise should take you on a journey of happiness and help you shift your energy towards positivity in a few minutes. You must allow yourself to be transported towards these journeys in life. Appreciate these feelings and be thankful for them. When you feel ready for this, take a deep breath in and exhale out. Repeat the breathing two more times. I would suggest practicing this outdoors on a sunny day and take any comfortable posture you prefer. Feel the warm sun on your face.

Feel the wind through your hair as if you are driving with your windows rolled down. Look at the world at a standstill as if it's 3 AM before the world awakens.

Imagine the sunrise over fields of colorful flowers. Close your eyes and imagine clear blue water surrounding the island of your dreams. Make up the sound of waves beating against a rocky beach. Recall the smell of damp soil after the first fall rain. Imagine the sound of leaves cracking beneath your feet as you walk through a forest. Imagine the warmth of a loved one's smile. Imagine the euphoric feeling you experience after you exercise.

Make up the relaxed feeling in your mind of a warm bath after a long day. Think of the warm and soft feeling left behind by your favorite cotton towel. Visualize the glow of a full moon at night. Feel the joy of a genuine compliment and the love from your loved ones. If you have a dog or a pet, imagine their love as you meditate. Make up the warmth of a hug in your mind. Imagine yourself eating your favorite foods and drinking your favorite drinks.

Imagine you being with friends and the connection of holding hands with someone you love and care about. Think of your favorite songs and why you love them. Think of your favorite color or your favorite piece of art. Imagine yourself dancing carelessly to your favorite song and being surrounded by your favorite people. Bring back the excitement you have before a holiday or a weekend getaway. Imagine yourself walking on warm wet sand on your favorite sandy beach. Imagine you are receiving your favorite relaxing massage. Recall the feeling of drinking a cold drink during a hot summer's day. Imagine a rainbow coming up after a stormy, rainy day, building itself up across the sky. Think of picturesque mountains across beautiful endless lakes of clear blue waters, with little wooden boats.

Imagine your favorite breed of puppies playing and having fun. Reminisce the time when a fire was cracking beneath slowly melting marshmallows on a breezy night. Think of waterfalls filling endless pools. Smell your favorite essential oil burning on your colorful burner. Enjoy the silence you are creating during this meditation exercise. Slowly bring yourself back to reality, knowing that your imagination or bringing back memories has brought so much happiness and joy to your day. Become aware of your body and slowly open your eyes.

Journaling

Journaling has been shown to aid with sadness, anxiety, and stress, according to research. Journaling can also assist you in coping with emotions, developing insights, reflecting on behavior or feelings, and recording important aspects of your life experience. Journaling is considered to assist you in acting as your own therapist. Another advantage of journaling is that it can help you focus on the creativity, beauty, connection, joy, and love in your life, which can increase your happiness.

If you've been journaling for a while, you already have a ton of knowledge sitting right under your nose. Your diary can educate you on how to be happier on those dreaded Mondays, how to deal with that nasty co-worker, how to ignore your hectic commute, how much your friends increase your happiness, and so on. There are over a thousand distinct ways to keep a journal. It's safe to anticipate that you won't like all the techniques. You'll need to choose a method of journaling that you enjoy. No one can tell you how to live a happy life, and no one can tell you which journaling style would bring you the most happiness.

But where do you begin? What should you be concentrating on? Do you write in a book, on a notepad, or on a computer? What exactly do you write about? How can you make keeping a notebook a habit? These may be challenging to answer, but they should not prevent you from getting started. The first step, like anything else, is typically the most difficult.

Everyone began the same way: by scribbling the first word on a scrap of paper. One of the most effective methods for being more thankful, attentive, self-aware, and introspective is journaling. These are my recommendations if you're not sure where to begin with, journaling: Purchase a cute pen. Start by sitting down with a cup of coffee and fill in the below questions EVERY morning and EVERY evening. This should take you no more than 5-minutes each time and be consistent. Consistency will help you evaluate your days and improve after each one.

MORNING JOURNALING

As soon as I woke up and came to my senses, I felt grateful for:

_____

_____

_____

_____

It would be great if today:

_____

_____

_____

_____

It would be great if today:

_____

_____

_____

_____

EVENING JOURNALING

Today was great because the following things happened:

_____

_____

_____

_____

What choices could I have made differently today for it to be better?

_____

_____

_____

_____

Have I achieved the goals set by myself this morning, today? If this did not happen, or not entirely, how can I improve this tomorrow?

_____

_____

_____

_____

Daily schedule

To help you maximize your day and feel better about it each day, here is a schedule I adopt for myself. This leaves me feeling content with my accomplishments even if I fail some things on my checklist. This is obviously something that cannot be a standard for everyone because you have commitments and a life you need to work around. Feel free to adjust this to fit your commute and your work schedule.

5:30 AM Wake up as soon as my alarm on my phone goes off. I leave my phone on my desk away from my bed the night before, so I am forced to wake up to switch it off and not snooze it.

5:45 AM I immediately make my bed, so this will further prevent me from sleeping in.

6:00 AM I boil some water in a kettle to prepare a warm cup of hot water with lemon. I start filling in the morning part of my journal while I drink my hot water.

6:30 AM I open my yoga mat and start my morning stretching yoga routine that only takes 10 minutes.

6:40 AM I change into the gym wear I laid out on the chair in my bedroom the night before. Fill me a bottle of water and wear my sports tracker. I head out for a jog. This can be a training session with whatever makeshift equipment you have at home or a session at the gym.

7:15 AM I return home to my beloved coffee machine, where I grind coffee beans and prepare my first espresso for the day. This is usually accompanied by a wholewheat ham and cheese toast and loaded with AT LEAST 3 types of vegetables. I sit down and enjoy my breakfast.

7:45 AM I start getting ready for work and head in the bathroom to have a shower. I get dressed and collect all the healthy snacks and lunches for the day. My commute to work usually takes me about 30 minutes on a good day.

8:45 AM I arrive at work, greet everyone, and head to my desk. Here I take out my diary with all the checklists I have created in my bed the night before. You may start ticking off some of them if they are work-related, or you may only start diminishing your lists right after work because your to-do list is made of errands outside of work.

1 PM At this time, I usually eat my lunch which typically includes another three different types of vegetables and a source of protein. I always leave a healthy sweet treat at the end to make me look forward to the rest of the day. I typically ensure I drink at least 2 liters of water. If, like me, you have a desk job, I usually opt to move away from my desk during lunchtime and, if possible, go outside.

5 PM My workday is over by this time, and I start heading out either at home or to wherever I need to be if I plan to run errands after work.

6 PM As soon as I arrive home, I start by putting things away to always maintain a clutter-free space. I go on preparing my snacks and lunches for the next day if not already done and prepare dinner also.

6:30 PM I take another 60 minutes of my day to train. This can vary from a home workout to an online class.

7:30 PM I eat dinner, and if I am due to watch my favorite season, this is the time I usually put that on to maximize my time.

8:15 PM I prepare myself for bed by taking a shower and getting my gym wear ready for the next morning. Before I get in bed, I play my favorite instrument for at least 15 minutes. I head into the bed and take out my diary. I start writing my checklists for the next day, so I know exactly what I plan to do. This way, I am prepared for the day ahead and inarguably set myself up for another successful day. When I plan my day down to the minute, I know what to do with my time, and I will feel more accomplished by the end of it.

9 PM I close my checklist diary and open my journal, and I evaluate my day by filling the evening bit of the day. I set the alarm for the next day and leave my phone to charge away from my bed. I then start by reading for the next 30 minutes. By this time, I would start feeling sleepy, so I close my book and drift into my comfy pillow.

Here are some things you can notice from the above schedule, and these things should be included in your schedule too, so keep them in mind whilst planning:

- ☑ No screen time right before bed
- ☑ Eight hours of sleep
- ☑ A healthy balanced diet with healthy prepared snacks at home and various vegetables or sources of protein included

- ☑ One hour+ of physical activity every day split into sessions
- ☑ Meditation, positive affirmations, yoga, or stretching daily
- ☑ Journaling daily
- ☑ Creating checklists every day
- ☑ Meal prepping daily and daily chores done
- ☑ Scheduling the next day ahead of time
- ☑ Give importance to "me-time" every day through meditation, reading, playing my favorite instrument, preparing my favorite drink (Coffee), and taking a relaxing shower/ bath at the end of the day
- ☑ Leaving time for commuting to always make it on time without rushing. Being late can make you feel rushed, panicked, and stressed.
- ☑ Maximization of my time, for example, watching my favorite episodes whilst eating.
- ☑ Allowing myself a lunch break away from my desk and outside whenever possible.
- ☑ Be 100% honest in my journaling and 100% realistic in my checklists keeping in mind the available time I have each day. Setting unrealistic goals can only make you feel unaccomplished and give you the notion of failure. This is the last thing you want for a joyful day.

Having the above schedule prepared every day is a blessing, to say the least. Every morning I wake up feeling thrilled for the day ahead, knowing I am prepared for what is to come. At the end of it all, I feel accomplished whether I had a bad day, had a colleague make me lose my temper, had a rough commute stuck in traffic, or not doing so well during a presentation at work.

At the end of it all, I always have a meal to look forward to, a healthy and delicious snack to munch on, a training session I cannot wait for because of the way I know it will make me feel afterwards, and at the end of it all I know I will return to a clean and tidy place to call my own, with another chance to re-live a better day the next morning.

CONCLUSION

Your personal health shouldn't be a riddle. Know what works for you and get rid of the obstacles that are keeping you from being happy. Be happy with the decisions you've made in your life; it is essential to your health and well-being. Happiness and good health are inextricably linked. Happiness may, in fact, make our hearts healthier, our immune systems stronger, and our lives longer, according to scientific research. Happiness is the purpose of life, as well as the entire goal of human existence.

The feeling of pleasant emotions such as joy, contentment, and satisfaction is referred to as happiness. According to new research, being happy not only makes you feel better, but it also has other health advantages. The universe revolves around happiness, or rather the lack thereof. It is one of the most desirable feelings in life. Many of our pursuits are made with the ultimate objective of bringing us closer to happiness.

Happiness is a personal experience, but it isn't rocket science. We overcomplicate things when they don't need to be so complex. The alternatives I've described here aren't unfathomable. They are the basic things you may do daily to boost your happiness level. Do not inquire as to what the world requires. Find out what makes you happy and then do it.

Many individuals are aware of the steps they must take to improve their chances of feeling happy. They sometimes find fulfillment by adhering to certain behaviors. They forget and become upset at times. Then it's time to reclaim control of their life. One strategy is to do activities in your personal and professional life that generate positive energy. The next stage is to repeat these procedures until they become second nature. Of course, you'll go about it your own way.

Instead of being angry, resentful, or obsessed with my past experiences, I now feel as though much good has come from everything. I've formed wonderful friendships with people who have stood by me during difficult times, and I'm confident in my capacity to overcome obstacles. I found the silver lining in the storm somewhere along the way, and you can as well.

Consider your life and the different obstacles you've overcome, as well as the numerous rewards you've reaped. By simply shifting your viewpoint and identifying the positive aspects of each situation, you can find the bright side of any scenario no matter how challenging it looks.

Keep in mind that changing your perspective is comparable to changing the window through which you view the world. When you change your vision of the world, your feelings about it change as well. It is possible that life will be challenging; nobody is spared from suffering. We all come across it at some point.

Remind yourself that the difficulties may be tough, but they will pass. Now dig deep to find purpose in your suffering. Choose to look for the advantages that your personal trial has to offer. At the very least, perseverance is being developed. And more than likely, the skill to console others in their distress is being cultivated as well.

We've looked at several ways you can streamline your calendar and reduce the amount of work you must finish. We discussed how to get organized, grow comfortable with saying no, and prioritize quality over quantity in relation to how and where you spend your time. You're careful and intentional about what you say "yes" to. You're making decisions to clear out space on your calendar so you can devote more time to the things that make you happy and you value the most.

This is what simplifying life is all about: getting rid of the clutter that prevents you from living your best life. Most of our objectives are geared around achieving some form of happiness. The final objective of every activity is happiness whether it's landing a great career, finding a loving relationship, or cooking the perfect egg. Our greatest efforts to uncover it, however, only serve to dig us deeper into depression.

Experiencing happiness today might assist you in having fewer regrets tomorrow. You'll have the guts to live the life you desire, rather than the one that others want for you. You'll figure out how to work less and have more joy. You'll have the confidence to express your emotions and be yourself. Because building a positive community to keep you happy takes time and work, you'll learn to remain in touch with your closest relatives and friends. All these factors will help you to become happier. You now have better insight into the reasons and methods that cause us to undermine our own happiness.

Now that we have come to an end of this life-changing workbook, do you feel that you have achieved the goals you listed at the beginning of the book? What strategies do you have in mind to cope with the struggle you have with happiness?

You have all the tools you need to BE happy and make it a permanent state in your life. Reread the book as many times as you need but know that everything you need is within an arm's reach! This is your final CHALLENGE, so do what you came here to do: BE HAPPY !

AUTHOR'S NOTE

Dear reader, I hope you enjoyed my book.

Please don't forget to toss up a quick review on amazon, I will personally read it! Positive or negative, I'm grateful for all feedback.

Reviews are so helpful for self-published authors and your feedback can make such a difference for my book!

Thanks very much for your time, and I look forward to hearing from you soon.

Sincerely,
Victoria

www.ingramcontent.com/pod-product-compliance
Lightning Source LLC
Chambersburg PA
CBHW080623030426
42336CB00018B/3057